CW00673828

Chasing More and Finding Enough

HOW BEING IS THE GREATEST FOUNDATION FOR EVERYTHING YOU DO

Arjuna Ishaya

FISHER KING

Chasing More and Finding Enough

Copyright © Arjuna Ishaya 2021

Paperback ISBN 978-1-913170-98-1
Ebook ISBN 978-1-913170-99-8

All rights reserved. No part of this publication may be reproduced or distributed in any form or by any means, or stored in a database or electronic retrieval system without the prior written permission of Fisher King Publishing Ltd.

The right of Arjuna Ishaya to be identified as the author of this work has been asserted by him in accordance with the Copyright, Designs and Patents act, 1988.

Thank you for respecting the author of this work.

Fisher King Publishing
The Old Barn
York Road
Thirsk
YO7 3AD
England
www.fisherkingpublishing.co.uk

www.arjunaishaya.com

www.thebrightpath.com

ACKNOWLEDGEMENTS

Standing on the shoulders of giants.

To my lovely Sumati for holding everything together while I put this together. You are amazing.

To Maharishi: not only did you teach me that struggle and suffering is not an inevitable part of being human, you showed me.

Thank you!
and go well,
Arjuna ☺

Thank you...

To Savitri for your beautiful job editing and advising, and for being an incredible cheerleader. You're awesome. To Dharani for your expertise, you are so appreciated. Tapas, you have an eagle's eye and artist's heart. Thank you so much for applying both to this.

To Anne Brady, Richard Crow, Steven D'Souza and Simon Gwilliam – for all your feedback that made this book what it is. I can't tell you how grateful I am for your time and care.

To Rick Armstrong for your support and faith in me.

And big gratitude to you, for reading this book. May it make a difference to your life.

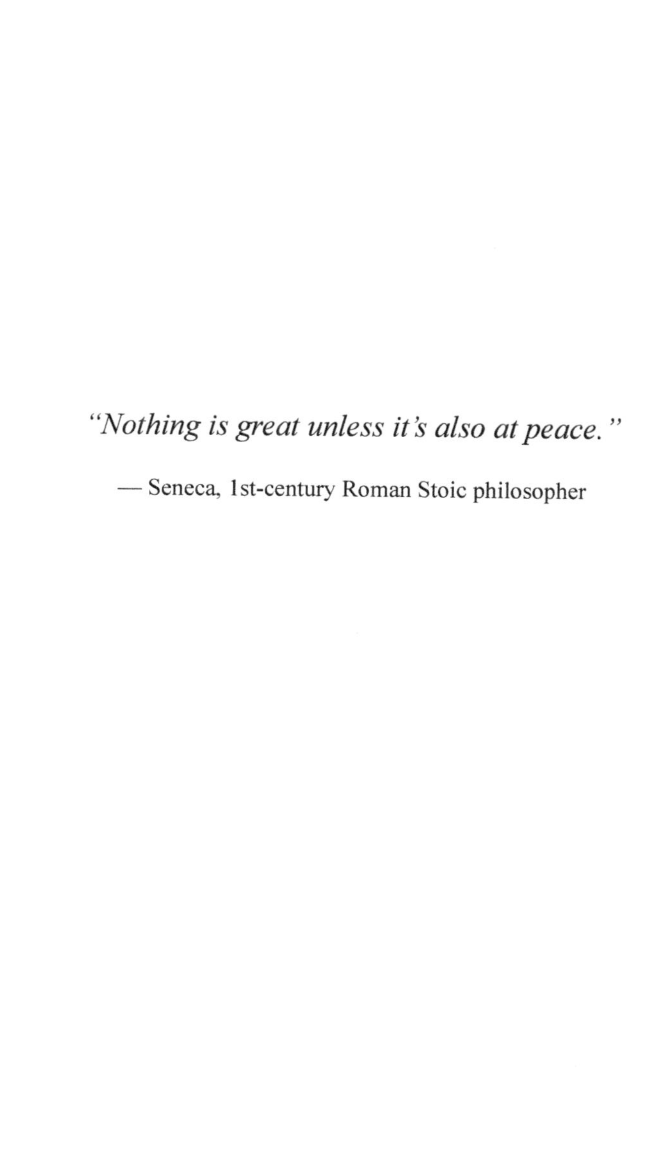

"Nothing is great unless it's also at peace."

— Seneca, 1st-century Roman Stoic philosopher

Contents

PREFACE

Find Fullness, Embrace the Opposite

"God turns you from one feeling to another and teaches by means of opposites, so that you will have two wings to fly, not one."

— Rumi, 13th-century Persian poet and mystic

Chasing more and finding enough: ambition and contentment, performance and peace, action packed doing and being chilled out... this is a book that could be about opposites.

Except it's not.

Our Western culture likes to put things in a box, carefully separated away from its apparent other. We love neatly contrasting ideas. We love to divide and separate: male or female, black or white, us or them, mind or body, hard or soft, culture or nature, order or chaos, logic or emotion, change or acceptance, courage or serenity, action or stillness.

We break down our worlds into opposites and then pick a side – and we are very much the lesser for this way of thinking. We become imbalanced, we miss out. We limit ourselves to 50% of life. While half a life is better than nothing, it's not great either.

Not only do we become a limited version of ourselves in trying to live up to these rigid definitions, it causes such internal self-doubt and confusion as the experience of life in all its shades and textures crashes against the binary black and white boxes of our belief systems.

We are deeply uncomfortable with life's shades of colour; we don't do well with embracing opposites. And this means we suffer.

It seems there has never been more anxiety and mental imbalance, anger and conflict, hopelessness and overwhelm. Our rigid thinking means we have difficulty dealing with change, and these are rapidly changing times. This is not the world our parents grew up in; it's possibly not even the world our older siblings and cousins found their way in.

We're searching for answers. We want to know who to be and what to do, definitely and absolutely, in order to navigate and get what we want from life. But the absolute answer to that question is: "It depends."

There is no one answer. It always depends. There are times when you need to switch on. There are times when you need to switch off. Flexibility, not rigidity, is required. Openness is key – to be calm and centred so that wisdom and intuition can show you the right thing to do, and when.

Fluidity, adaptability, understanding, perspective,

present and alive awareness... these are the sources of the clear, inspired insight we are looking for – but without throwing away the ability to tap into, when needed, the traditionally valued head-down drive, discipline, determination and ability to get things done.

But here we're talking a kind of doing that has a smile in its heart: joyful, flowing, satisfying action, packed with presence and Being. Such a different beast from that based in struggle, pushiness, impatience, need, fear.

What we're talking about here is not either/or. It's both. It's "Yes, *and...*". This, therefore, is a book about comprehending the fullness of life: not settling for half a life but finding all of it.

It's about broadening your horizons, embracing opposites and getting rid of either/or thinking. It's also about narrowing your horizons and tuning into what the moment in front of you requires. It's about finding an anchor you can truly live from, where uncertainty, challenge and chaos can't rock your ship.

This is a book about more than merely coping or becoming "resilient". It's about the end of the dissatisfaction, emptiness and suffering that is at the core of a huge amount of our lives – even those of us who seem to have it all.

It's about finding a completely different approach to

achieving your ambitions and making your life – and the world – better. A life that is free of overwhelm and negativity, reaction and conflict; one that is inspired and powerful, bold and authentic, compassionate and useful, fulfilled and complete.

This is a spiritual book that wants you to have your cake and eat it too; that says the only things you need to renounce in order to enjoy the benefits of an inner path is limitation itself.

I don't care who you are and what you do: I say you're a lover of life. This is a book that wants you to have more, to be truly able, effective, and alive – and the foundation for this begins with the willingness to embrace the paradox that your ability to chase more is only amplified through finding enough.

It's about Greek philosopher Aristotle's maxim that, "The whole is greater than the sum of its parts". Having two wings to fly means you can truly soar further and higher.

Let's go.

INTRODUCTION

The Donut Life

"Yes, but I have something he will never have...
Enough."

— Joseph Heller in reply to gossip that the billionaire host of a party he was attending had made more money in one day than Heller had earned from his most popular novel, Catch 22, in its whole history.

By my late twenties, I had made an incredible life in my homeland of New Zealand. I was an outdoor instructor – in the summer I'd kayak and run and climb mountains, in the winter I'd snowboard. I think I got more than one hundred days riding one winter, which isn't too bad at all.

Where I was living, the very cool jobs, the friends, the adventures, the goals I was ticking off... they were all amazing. And yet it didn't add up to much either. Author Steven Pressfield could have been talking about me when he wrote, "Our days were simultaneously full to the bursting point and achingly, heartbreakingly empty".

I was so confused. Why? I had everything, but it seemed like I had nothing, nothing of true importance.

Except sometimes the Zen moments would come, and it didn't seem to matter what I was doing. Maybe I was kayaking or snowboarding, maybe sipping tea in the sun on my back doorstep, maybe I was at work or some social event. But the change in me was always profound.

A simple yet deep and complete sense of okay-ness would embrace me. Ease. The striving to secure and control would cease. Nothing needed; all that was left was fullness, a dropping of any kind of guard, an unspoken approval for – and satisfaction in – my existence and the moment.

Peace.

In peace I found a wonderful version of me. Not trying to be someone I wasn't. Free of evaluation or self-management, agitation or regret. Not seeking to be somewhere else. Simply content to be alive, communing with life as I found it.

When I was outdoors, this peace would combine with a pure physical prowess, where doing became almost effortless. I was given the almost magical ability to meet the exact need of the moment: reflexes sharp, doubts gone, everything coming together. And all complete with a joyful appreciation for the playful act of doing.

This is what I was looking for – this felt like I was truly alive!

But these treasured Zen moments didn't seem to happen enough, they ended too soon, and I didn't know how to get them back. It seemed the only constant was the persistent mental chatter, the anxious, doubting and dissatisfied voice going on between my ears. I had so much to enjoy, yet none of it gave me anything lasting.

I felt like a donut: I had a beautiful life on the outside, but nothing on the inside.

But how could I even complain? I had precisely arranged my life, I had achieved my version of success, and yet this didn't feel like success... it felt empty.

"Poor me", I hear you say, and I get it. But if you don't have a concrete inner connection with anything truly significant, it doesn't matter if you're on top of the pile or at the bottom. Being a donut is not fun. That kind of emptiness is tough.

No matter what you throw into the void, it never fills up. Nothing: careers, cars, expensive dining, shoes, adventures and holidays. Not sex, drugs, rock and roll and risk... none of it satisfies.

No matter how hard you work to achieve more to shovel into the hole, none of it can make you whole. Nothing material can give you fulfilment that lasts. No amount of more can ever be enough.

Why? Because enough is never caused. It is chosen. It comes via an inner connection with your sense of Being. It is Being that brings wholeness, peace and satisfaction, not all the doing and getting and endlessly chasing more we get lost in.

We are Human Beings First

Buddha supposedly once said, "You only suffer when you forget who you truly are". Whoever actually said it, they hit the nail on the head.

We are great Do-ers. However, we are human beings first, not human doings. When we forget our Being, the result is always a void – and suffering.

Without Being we can't enjoy any of our work, and there is no real basis for achievement either. A house needs a foundation and walls before you can bring in the couch, TV and coffee machine; the finest wine needs a glass before you can enjoy it; there can be no movement without something unmoving to push against. Similarly, the completeness of Being gives us the structure to live from.

Being is the experience of your presence, the sense of your inner existence, the lived fact of your aliveness. You could call it soul, spirit, or your higher Self. It does not do, it just *is*. But it is the source of all inspiration and joy, passion and creation, fulfilment and meaning. It is the source of quality: that sense of rightness, of good, of beauty and integrity and truth. Being is the source of all wisdom and clarity. It inspires and nourishes and shines forth from everything we do. It is quite ungraspable and immeasurable, yet it is more real than anything else on this planet.

There's an old saying, "Go within, or go without". We neglect forming a relationship with our Being at our peril. But by putting Being first, we have the source of everything at our disposal. Going within means you can go beyond.

Being is the context to the content of our work, the end of doubt and fear, the giver of stability and structure and certainty in an ever-changing and chaotic world. It is patience and purpose and peace. It is Home. Don't leave home without it. Don't even get out of bed.

Now –

Not for a second am I suggesting you stop having goals or looking after your responsibilities. This is not about renouncing ambition and a chase for more, it isn't about making either/or decisions. As meditation teacher Jack Kornfield says, "You need to remember your Buddha nature *and* your social security number".

Recognise too that this isn't so much about balance, like balancing alternating periods of doing and Being, like swapping out work and recovery – although that is useful. But it is about making first things, first. It is about making Being the foundation of everything you do.

Many of us reading this might have a hard time getting our heads around that to begin with. I certainly did. This is not what our culture teaches us, and it's why our experiences of finding enough are so rare, and so fleeting. But we've all had a taste of it, I'm sure.

How do we get more, without struggle and strain, grasping and grabbing? For, as I found, pushing too hard is a sure way of *not* getting more.

Pushing Too Hard

Short-lived as my perfect Zen moments were, they brought so much satisfaction, aliveness and enough (and a total contrast to my Donut Life existence), they fuelled a quest to find more of them.

Looking back, I realised that my best performances as a young competitive swimmer in my teens came when I embodied Being. When I had no care for the end result; when I was excited to turn up and see what was about to unfold; when I wasn't focused on, and anxious about, the gold medal, but in simply taking care of the exact present moment I found myself in.

I started to see that when I stopped trying so damn hard to get something or somewhere, it all came together – which is perverse to our usual way of thinking, isn't it? Yet the more I lived and experienced, the more I saw the benefit and beauty of this kind of non-grasping, non-trying, non-doing approach.

In studying for my Masters degree I did nothing hard, no punishing schedules – I agreed with myself that I'd only go to the office when I felt like it and walk away when I didn't – and yet more great work, in less time with more joy, got done than I had ever experienced in my life.

On the river, the presence of a camera and the opportunity

to show the world evidence of my kayaking brilliance only produced rigidity and tension. In the footage it was crystal clear that I was in my head and not in my body. In the grasping for my best and to stand out, I got my worst.

When I'd go out on the town in my early twenties looking to meet someone, the times I would have the best conversations and the best connections was when I had nothing to lose. When I wasn't expecting anything, when I wasn't *trying* to be somebody, I felt women would throw themselves at me.

Our egos love to claim achievement for themselves; they love to be seen. They will try anything to gain recognition. And yet, this is so un-appealing. Maybe, like me, you've found that humility and modesty are highly attractive, almost magnetic, in others? Arrogance and, "Look at me, I'm someone impressive" repels. It does the opposite. When you're content to be nobody, not trying to be someone, everyone is drawn to you. Curious, huh?

In my writing, I can't push. As soon as I do, as soon as it feels like hard work, the quality drops. If I push, I have to redo. And it's no fun to struggle to produce the next words. They come best when I let them. Of course, I have to show up to my computer. That's something I do, but the rest, I can't do.

Life – and performance – was clearly better for me when I didn't try, when I didn't force or struggle. When I wasn't attached to more, I got more than plenty.

I saw time and time again that struggle resulted in less. Contentment, I felt, was the path to effortlessness, and effortlessness meant that super high quality moments could come, free of strain, overwhelm, or negativity.

Perhaps most importantly, I found that my sense of self and self-esteem – the judgement of the quality of my Being – was deeper than something I did or didn't do. It was a fact, independent of my achievements, or my mistakes. It was something real, something lasting, something true – regardless of my results, of what people thought of me, or what I even thought of myself.

The times when I was without Being, my inner voice of self-criticism was brutal about the deficiencies and mistakes it found. But the times when I was centred and aligned, all – including me – was well. I can't tell you the relief to be content in my own skin. But perhaps you've had a taste of that too?

Yet we in the West aren't conditioned to think like this, to structure our lives like this, to be like this. And it's a shame. There is so much more to be found from life when we let go of our death-grip on doing and struggling to get more; when we stop focusing solely on future goals and rewards. I found this out the hard way.

Sacrifice Now, Heaven Later

My swimming coach often talked about mental toughness. I soaked this up, aiming to embody the fortitude and resilience that I thought was needed to plow through obstacles, to put in the extra mile, to push through when everyone else gave up.

"Practice makes perfect" was the idea: the harder and longer I worked, the more I would succeed. Right? And by no means was I the only one with this philosophy; our whole culture is founded on it. We are saturated in the Protestant work ethic: work hard and long, sacrifice now, attain your dreams later on. Deny now, Heaven later.

We see rest as the reward for hard work, peace as the end result of performance. Performance, achieving, and getting – that's what earns you ease, completeness, contentment, and fulfilment; the sense of satisfaction of a job well done. More, we believe, can create a feeling of enough.

And it's true. Nothing happens without action, devotion, commitment and work, and it is so fulfilling to invest time and effort into something and have it come off.

We are never happier than when it feels like we are moving forward in life. Making plans, having dreams, and achieving goals: ticking things off your list, and making a difference – it's a key part of life. Having meaningful work, contributing, growing... not only is all of this an important part of mental health and wellbeing, it's an important part of thriving and truly feeling alive.

As the 19th-century philosopher Friedrich Nietzsche once wrote, "Joy is the feeling of one's powers increasing". Performance psychologist Mihaly Csikszentmihalyi also talks about the importance of challenge and growth, to anyone:

"These periods of struggling to overcome challenges are what people find to be the most enjoyable of their lives. A person who has achieved control over psychic energy and has invested it in consciously chosen goals cannot help but grow into a more complex being. By stretching skills, by reaching toward higher challenges, such a person becomes an increasingly extraordinary individual."

Having a desire for more is important. Don't throw that away. Avoidance of action and not going towards anything is not the answer to the kind of life you're looking for. The trouble is, however, we take this focus on chasing more to unbalanced and exhausting extremes.

We in the West have a culture that is top heavy on doing, getting, achieving, goals. On growing, transforming, becoming. On the future, on what's next and what's new.

You could argue that the basis of our whole economic system of capitalism is making sure the graph keeps climbing: never-ending growth. No wonder we are so obsessed with getting more and the new and different. Having enough, on the other hand, is not good for business.

We are not a culture of contentment, appreciation, presence, spirit, Being. Nor are we big on choosing to have enough. We aren't a culture of rest, of enjoying, of stopping to smell the roses.

There's a strong Puritan streak, still. Those cultures who take long leisurely lunches and siestas like France and Spain? Those with a super-relaxed and undemanding sense of "Island time" like in the Pacific or Caribbean? We paint them as lazy non-achievers, possibly as we're unconsciously jealous, wishing we had the courage to let go of the obsession with chasing more to the same extent.

But I say we need to.

While discipline, denial and discomfort have their place, our culture's extreme relationship with more means so many of us take them too far. We whole-heartedly embrace the idea that if anything is worth doing, it's worth over-doing. More is always seen as better, so we don't do as much as is needed, we do as much as possible.

And this imbalanced approach has consequences.

I crashed out of swimming with a shoulder injury at the ripe old age of 17 – my sole focus on mental toughness and working harder didn't take long to blow up on me physically. A similarly idealistic and hard-charging triathlete on my team – with a heart condition that he knew about – *died* during a race. We had met the truth of an old Chinese proverb, "A tree that is unbending is easily broken". There was little or no yin to our yang, no water to our steel, no stop to our go, no Being to our doing.

It wasn't just physical damage. Spending more time in the physio's office than in the water, I judged myself a washed up failure. My whole sense of identity was wrapped up in performing in the pool.

My self-esteem, my sense of Being was completely linked to achievement, high performance, and hard work itself – I had nothing, no reference point, no sense of Self outside of that.

It's a common thing among athletes, even those who are successful and can retire at the pinnacle of their careers. Depression, anxiety, even suicide, are rampant among the highest of sporting performers. A big part of this is due to the fact that when you finish, no number of gold medals and records can fill the hole left by the disappearance of who you thought you were.

It was a tough experience, but ultimately a liberating one because it made me find balance and a fullness and completeness to life that was missing. And I'm not the only one to have experienced this problem. I've been talking about my experience in sports, but I see this everywhere. We're all suffering in some way for a lack of balance.

What exactly is the problem? And how did the world get in such a mess?

PART ONE: THE PROBLEM

The Cost of Valuing More Most

Look and you will see what it costs us to be so excellent at doing and chasing more and so useless at Being and choosing to enjoy enough. There's burnout, overwhelm, negativity everywhere. Our physical and mental health is suffering, our relationships are suffering, our enjoyment of life is suffering, society itself is suffering.

Stress is now considered *the* currency of getting things done, of taking care of business. My brother, a high level banker, and I were talking about our different points of view on stress. "I get paid to be stressed", he said. "No, you don't", I countered, "You get paid to be responsible. There's a vast difference". Now I'm obviously making myself appear a lot wiser in this recreation, but you get the point: stress is seen as the necessary price you pay if you want to play in the world of goals and achieving. Yet stress is also the biggest cost to companies and governments in terms of ill health, days off sick, and worker dissatisfaction.

Mindfulness is still huge because everyone's heads are running amok from all the doings we think we need to think about. We are frantically running in circles, overwhelmed at the scale of the work and our To-Do lists. We're plugged in 24/7. We're checking – and responding to – work emails and message groups late into the night and on holiday. We can't sleep, our attention spans are counted in seconds, we can't stop and do nothing. In the irony of ironies, we're so focused on chasing more and the new and different that our ability to effectively do just that has gone down the drain.

Anxiety is wildly out of control. Walking down the street the other day I saw a mother helping her daughter through a panic attack by reminding her to take deep breaths. The girl was still in pigtails; she can't have been 10 years old.

Depression, loneliness, self-harming, eating disorders, addictions, suicide and other diseases of despair are rife. Pornography is more available than ever before, yet sexual satisfaction has never been so low. We have plentiful access to more food than ever before, yet we can't get enough. We have never been so obese.

The technical revolution of the future promised more leisure time for everyone, but now we're here? We feel like we have less time than ever.

We're more connected via social media, but there's less empathy and understanding. We're becoming more socially siloed, more tribal, more blinkered and extreme in our beliefs. Conspiracy theories are everywhere and taken seriously by big chunks of the population – and it's just the tip of the iceberg.

The chase for more has been pushed so much above all

other things, and we're just starting to see the fallout. It's becoming so any kind of decency or humanity or morality or integrity that would get in the way of getting more is discarded as a hindrance.

"Greed is good!" says capitalist baron Gordon Gekko – an ultimate expression of material achievement from Oliver Stone's 1987 film Wall Street. While Gekko gets his comeuppance, increasing numbers of people today think selling your soul to get what you want is a wonderful exchange.

Witness our political parties' current relationship with facts and the truth: "Do whatever it takes to win – nothing else matters" is the manifesto, no matter the havoc that kind of philosophy causes.

What use is something like the quality of your character, your Being, when you can taste victory?

But as Jesus warned about the blinkered pursuit of material more thousands of years ago: "What good will it be for someone to gain the whole world, yet lose their very self?".

The Greatest Problem

Perhaps the greatest problem is our either/or, black and white, binary and opposite way of thinking about ourselves and the world.

While we see performance as dynamic, making your way in the world, achieving your goals, chasing more, peace is believed to mean complacency, getting soft, losing your drive. If you want to give up your dreams and what you want in life, the fastest way would be to embrace peace and feel you have enough, we are told. We believe the contentment found in enough is giving up. It's checking out and slacking off and not being responsible.

I've lost count of how many times I've talked with great Do-ers like entrepreneurs, athletes and the military who've turned their noses up at meditation or any kind of inner journey: "I don't want to lose my edge", they say. "I don't want to dull my aggression." All well and good, and they might seem to be doing well, but only in one sphere of their lives, usually work. There's no balance. The rest – their relationships, their health, their ability to switch off or enjoy anything else – is so often a mess.

We have become so focused on doing to the detriment of our well-being. Author Anna Quindlen spoke about this:

"People don't talk about the soul very much anymore. It's so much easier to write a résumé than to craft a spirit. But a résumé is cold comfort on a winter night, or when you're sad, or broke, or lonely, or when you've gotten back the chest X-ray and it doesn't look so good, or when the doctor writes 'prognosis, poor'...

You cannot be really first-rate at your work if your work is all you are."

Our way of seeing things separates the spiritual, inner world path of peace and Being from the material, outer world chase for performance and doing. The monk lives in a completely different reality from the businesswoman, the athlete or the lover of life... or so we believe.

We think we have to choose a path in life, either/or. Which will it be? Take care of your responsibilities and make something of yourself, or throw in the towel to take an inner, spiritual path and waste your life, gazing at your navel?

Who in their right mind would give up the beauty, the fun, the achievement and the adventures to be had out in the world by locking themselves away from sensory pleasure in order to find peace? (Not that you have to, but that's the way the story goes.)

Pick one, we're told. Choose! Peace, contentment, and a spiritual path? Or, performance, action, achieving and enjoying what the world has to offer?

I really wanted more Zen moments, but there was no way I was going to exchange peace for the joys of the world, that was for sure. So the decision was easy, in one sense. Yet we're choosing for a false division, something we don't need to choose between – and that only creates problems, it creates half a life.

On some level we know this. Like me, many of you will suspect there's something else, something missing – "What am I doing wrong?", or even, "What's the point?" we may ask ourselves when we really feel empty – but so complete is our cultural conditioning we can't quite put our finger on it. We're dissatisfied but don't know why. We can feel like we have so much, but *are* so little.

Devoid of any real answers, we get through the Donut Life as best we can. "Mustn't complain", we tell ourselves... and yet the feeling we're missing something important is still there, nagging, just beyond reach.

Some of us – and this is a blessing though in the beginning it may feel like a curse – even hear this nagging as an actual voice. Out of the blue it would call me by name; sometimes just that, other times with, "What are you doing?" or "Wake up!". Weird, right? Though not as weird as talking back. "Shut the hell up!" I'd yell, mainly because the voice was affirming that those quiet yet nagging doubts were true.

It doesn't matter if you get this voice or not. It doesn't matter whether you feel like there's something missing, or actually, you feel life is pretty good. You can have more. Often there's so little to show us a different way of living, so let me say this again:

It's not an either/or choice! You *can* have both. Peace creates the conditions for true performance and mastery, Being provides the structure for all our doings, it is finding enough that allows us to joyfully chase more.

Take a whole approach and you find balance, completeness and the lived answer to any frustrating questions of "What am I missing?". Embrace these seeming opposites and you end stress, struggle and suffering. You gain the secret to an exceptional life: not just doing okay, but *flourishing*.

We Think Peace is Caused, Not Chosen

So – we think: work hard, do well, get rewarded, and rest. Achieve, then you can let go. Peace, contentment, satisfaction... these are seen as the end-products of achieving more. Peace, we believe, is caused. It's a result, it's something different happening: losing weight, your kids behaving, doing something you love, politicians saying something you agree with, winning that medal, finishing that project.

Chasing more and chasing results, as I said, can be a wonderful thing, but it's become an addiction: it's not a want, it's a *need*. We need to achieve and to become because without it, we feel we'll never have enough to fill the void in our lives.

Now, I'm not talking about the necessary tactic of delaying gratification. I'm talking about the fact that since we believe peace is *caused*, we're less and less able to *choose* to be at peace, regardless of the circumstances in our lives. We are unable to be content, exactly as we are and as the world is, because we believe peace is caused by everything in our life – the people, the events, the circumstances – all perfectly lining up the way we want them to.

We become victims to these external circumstances and to other people. "I will be happy when...". When your boss treats you fairly? When your partner is a certain way? When your football team wins? When rainy days stop? But who has ever had their lives arranged perfectly for more than a day or two? No one.

Even when we tick off a significant goal, many of us can only soak in the satisfaction of accomplishment for about two seconds before our hyper-critical, more-oriented brains move onto what we did wrong and how we could have done it better – or what we need to achieve next.

Peace becomes this difficult to obtain, and impossible to maintain, end result of perfection. And yet we still pursue it. We attach to life looking a certain way. "I will be happy when..." easily becomes, "I can *only* be happy when...".

For me, "only happy when" showed up mostly in chasing the high of my precious Zen moments in the outdoors. They became an addiction – anything less was hollow and disappointing: just not good enough. Anything less "made" me grumpy, frustrated, dissatisfied – for *days*. So I pushed harder; and the harder I pushed, the more the proverbial wet bar of soap slipped from my grasp. The more I forced and grabbed, the less Zen I got.

I would fume, even yell, and I'm kind of ashamed of who I became – just like a little child having a tantrum, throwing his toys. Yuck. Instead of being able to choose to be content with what I had, I couldn't enjoy my time in my favourite places with my favourite people. I could only be fulfilled *when...*

Even with everything I know today – in writing this book, if the words are coming smooth and easy, my mind says my day is amazing, awesome. If the writing is sticky and not so fluid, the day is terrible. I'm never going to create anything of value and I might as well burn it all now.

I've gotten a lot better at ignoring it, but our minds mean we're like a monkey on a chain – it seems we're not free to choose to be at peace. We're pulled to and fro, our whole mood coloured by one event.

You see how easily resistance and agitation and over-control and stress over what we dislike, or what "shouldn't be happening" comes in? Struggle and stress and not being the person we want to be happens because we believe if we don't make our lives the way we want them to be, we will never be happy and find enough.

Obviously there is much we can control, but there is so much more we can't. Control, therefore, is a poor strategy to try to achieve peace and satisfaction. Learn to choose for peace instead, no matter the circumstances. Don't let it be caused by something outside of you, or outside of your control.

And by the way, if you see any of this in yourself?

It's such a great thing. Because if you become aware of these unconscious habits, you can learn to choose differently. It means you won't let peace and happiness be caused by something outside of you, or outside of your control. It means you can free yourself of limitation and negativity – a wonderful thing, right? So, well done – you're on your way to Being and doing all of life better.

When/Then...

The trouble with "I will be happy when..." lies in the word "When".

You see, more and different always take time to create. Building and becoming is a journey. Achieving (and therefore caused peace and enough) is always a future moment.

When we are so focused on the top of the mountain that we're climbing, satisfaction is always up there, never here: enjoyment is upon completion. In the attachment caused by "I can only be happy when...", you can't appreciate what you have now.

In this, we are excellent time travellers – in looking for there we completely lose here.

For me, the When/Then problem mostly took the form of living for the weekend. I'd spend the whole week getting excited about Saturday and Sunday's adventure, and yet I'd waste a huge chunk of Sunday dreading the oncoming Monday and the start of work.

Work was always disappointing because it wasn't the weekend, and the weekend was over (in my head) far too soon. Ironically, my habit of living in the future meant I often had trouble applying myself to now. It could be tricky to immerse myself in the moment that

I'd spent all week anticipating; my head would be anywhere but here.

But when I did let go of what was coming next and give my full attention to what was happening in front of me, life – *regardless* if I was at work or play – really came alive. I could be totally content *and* completely tuned in to what was going on, no matter what the moment contained.

This is the secret to getting there with quality and style; without perpetually putting your life on hold for a future moment. Bring some here in exchange for a total focus on there, and you'll find you can enjoy each and every step on the journey to what's next. You can soak in, and be grateful for, what is around you.

See, the beauty of enough is that it needs no time to create. It's never about when, it's always a decision about now. It either is, or it's not. It's a choice. Can you be content with what is, now, while you work on what you wish to become or what's coming next? You can.

Enough is simply about being present and alive to this moment in time. It's parking the struggle for more and exchanging it for a relationship with this moment exactly as it is – and not when it looks like you insist it should.

Being means you don't *need* to create and achieve and become different to try to fulfil some lack, some hole in you – but you still most certainly want to create. The excitement for creation becomes, if anything, greater, and it's free of pressure and overwhelm because there's no attachment to it occurring or not.

You enjoy everything more because your satisfaction is here and now, but you're also more effective – you can shift your focus solely off a future prize and attend to what can be done, right now.

Useful huh?

Balance your chase for more with enough – with what is right in front of you. It's essential. In fact: without enough, there is no more. Ironic that, isn't it? The one thing that will bring us more with less struggle and more appreciation, is the one thing we cast aside for later, believed to be the end result of getting.

You Can Only Stop Doing When You're Done

If, as we think, peace is achieved and not chosen, the only place to rest is on your laurels. We believe we can only stop doing when we are done. Yet who has ever got to the end of their To-Do list? There is always more to do.

So we try working faster, we try multitasking, we try bulletproof coffee and nootropics and microdosing and waking up earlier – all so we can get things done, all so we can stop and be at peace.

Yet more is insatiable. You will always be asked for more. That's just a fact of life. We are never done. Peace, therefore, becomes an ever-shifting pot of gold at the end of our To-Do lists. No wonder so many of us feel like hamsters on a wheel.

We wake in the night with a million concerns, we make more lists, we get so busy thinking even when we're trying to enjoy down time: we're at home but we're actually still at work in our heads. But no matter how hard or fast we work, we never quite get there. The fundamental cause of our dissatisfaction remains: the focus on being done because we believe that will give us enough.

I had this very same moment of clarity in the middle

of arranging (what I thought was) an enormous project involving an international speaker, complete with media interviews and publicity, ticket sales, venue preparation... the whole convoluted works. My first time arranging something on this scale, my To-Do list was a mile long and it weighed heavy on my soul. Overwhelm and dread was kicking my butt, all day and all night.

One option for me was to quit. And saying "No" to more things can be a great strategy. But short of making a hermit of yourself, a big part of a fulfilling life is indeed chasing more. Again, don't reject that part of you entirely.

As I contemplated quitting, I realised that regardless of what I tried to do, my life will never be problem free. I could run, as they say, but I could never hide. Life will never be perfect, lined up as I wanted it to. There will always be more; I will never be done.

This project will end but another will come in its place – I will be asked to do other things that make me uncertain and uncomfortable or involve time pressure, *and* I'll put myself voluntarily in these positions. The refrigerator will always need restocking, more bills will come next month, the children may forever need attending to. There will always be people who I disagree with and rub me up the wrong way, there will always be bad news in the newspaper.

Avoidance wasn't an option – I saw I needed to learn to deal with it all differently.

I needed to find a sense of done in the middle of whatever imperfect mess I found myself in. I needed to find peace *with* unending chaos and challenge, with the partial and incomplete, with the uncomfortable and uncertain – otherwise I would kill myself through stress.

Short of trying to dodge challenge and responsibility – which is like trying to avoid life itself – I think we could all benefit from finding the same.

Learn to choose to find enough and peace here now, and not when you get there, to the goal, to the end. Learn to choose especially if you have the busiest and most demanding schedule, the tightest time pressures, the longest and most intense To-Do lists. In fact, as I said – you'll need to, because the only place to be done is when you're dead. There may you rest in peace.

So, find enough. It truly is either now, or never.

Don't Waste a Moment

One of the zeitgeists (the common spirit or mood) of our time is the quest to be, "The best version of you". When you look through your social media, you'll see it everywhere. You'll see such a chase for fulfilment through achievement: to create more, be more, become more. More is better!

In this extreme quest for self-improvement, there is such an emphasis on the hack, to optimise, to squeeze every moment and make it useful, to tweak it in the service of the pursuit of more. Slacking off and doing nothing doesn't seem to have a time or a place anymore.

Relaxing in some parts of the wellness space is sold as "recovery" – just long enough to get back on the treadmill. "Ready to get after it again, you go-getter?". What about just kicking back for the sheer joy of doing nothing, of enjoying freedom from striving, to simply be and enjoy your unmodified existence as it is?

I get it.

"You could DIE tomorrow!", "What are you doing with your life????", "Be your best self and make the most of your one precious life!" And what powerful reminders to stop procrastinating, to stop delaying, to understand that life *is* precious and to start living. That's what I want too. I want to squeeze everything I can from life, to not waste a single moment.

Yet this is also the age of rampant anxiety and depression. There is huge fear – of missing out, that we're not enough, that we're just not up to being the ideal superwoman or superman.

I lost count of how many people on paid leave I talked to during COVID lockdown who felt guilty for not taking all the spare time they had to learn Spanish, bake sourdough, or declutter and optimise their cupboard space. They felt guilty for crashing on the couch and resting... yet that's all they could do, so exhausted they were from the chase to do and become.

Perfectionism? Our culture means we hold so many expectations, demands, insistences on ourselves, with so little love and space to let what needs to happen to happen. There's so little gratitude for what we have. The focus on more and better means we can get myopic on what we need to do to become better, and forget the simplicity, and necessity, of enough and Being.

When are you good enough, as you are? In this desperate pursuit of caused peace and happiness through better and more, how many people are driven by fear that they are not enough?

Not Doing Enough – Not Being Enough

Aubrey Marcus, a well-known health/wellness author and podcaster who "built one of the fastest growing companies in America" (according to Google), once talked about having, "The constant, unending, unceasing anxiety that says you should be doing more, you're not doing enough".

Tim Ferriss, another hugely successful author/ podcaster, agrees. Ferriss also has material more, but he describes his achievements as being fuelled by self-loathing:

"I spent most of my life hating myself, at best tolerating myself for moments. There was a lot of self-loathing driving performance... [I] know plenty of achievers who are miserable, who are high performing, well-known people who are utterly miserable."

The Donut Life is the most frustrating and confusing thing in the world. You, by all popularly held measures are successful, and yet you're miserable. No matter what you have, without the ability to choose for enough you will never be okay and find enough, anywhere. Contentment and peace are continually elusive, no matter what you do.

The core of our suffering is because we evaluate our very Beings by our doings – or lack of doing. Doing becomes the sole source of your sense of Self and validation of your Being. Thinking "I'm not doing enough" easily means "*I am* not enough". But by what measuring stick? If we measure our worth solely by what we achieve... no wonder we're finding our Selves to be lacking.

When I dropped out of swimming, I had nothing else. I truly felt empty. It felt worse when I tried a comeback. I could never reach my former times and so quit again, feeling empty twice over. Even when I was older with (perhaps) a better sense of who I was, a great day out on the river meant I felt like the man. All was right in the world. When it didn't go so well, I was a failure, I was an idiot for wasting an opportunity. I needed to get out again pronto to prove myself, to myself.

How many talented and intelligent people drive themselves into misery and stress and ill-health, forever chasing more, forever trying to fill the hole of "I am not enough" with more and more achievement? How many amazing people are drowning under the weight of their own impossible expectations of themselves? How many wonderful people are more-or-less constantly insecure and neurotic because they're chasing perfection and completion, with no anchor in enough?

And so, we make a mistake... the unexamined images of

perfectionism we've swallowed mean the judgement, "I've done wrong" quickly becomes just further evidence that "I *am* wrong".

A mistake for me would result in the worst kind of punishment: constant mental and emotional self-torture. Any kind of perceived failure, weakness or even slight social awkwardness would result in an eternal review of what went wrong and what I needed to do differently and/or better, as well as how I could make up for my shame – what I might say or do to make amends.

Crazy huh? The crazy thing is a bunch of you know exactly what I'm talking about. And many of us had the blessing of never growing up with social media and its constantly available, and impossibly polished, showroom of success to compare our lives unfavourably with.

The result of all this?

We either: 1). Punish ourselves, driving ourselves harder and harder, digging the hole deeper and deeper; or, 2). We quit in disgust.

Us quitters often never show up again for fear of making a mistake, for fear of being reminded of how wrong we actually are. We never try what we might, sitting in self-loathing and self-resentment until we can find something mediocre we might not fail at, something we can make do with.

The mountain of more and becoming can be so intimidating for some of us even to begin climbing, it can be easier to give up the whole project. So jaded are we of feeling like we are wrong, we'd rather stay safe and cozy and unchallenged than be reminded of this belief.

So many of us are afraid of growth, of learning, of change. We just don't want to change. Change is threatening, it's uncomfortable. We don't want to be provoked and awoken. We don't want to do any more than we have to.

We just want to know that we're okay as we are. We want to know we're enough. We want to believe that we're not broken and lacking, and it seems sometimes self-doubt and self-criticism is easier to make disappear by giving up any attempt to become.

In this quest to feel okay and secure, to not feel wrong, to lessen the hugeness of our self-improvement To-Do lists, we lower our standards, we sedate and self-soothe, we ignore, we try to hide. Because we think we are what we do, if we don't try we can't fail, and that, we think, might be enough for one lifetime.

One of the biggest regrets of those in old age though?

It's not failing or making a mistake or appearing a fool in front of your peers. It's having an idea or a dream and being so scared of failure and feeling that we are wrong that we don't try.

Before the obvious inevitability of the deadline of death dawns on us, the mantra easily becomes for so many, "I give up. Just entertain me. Let me forget, let me be comfortable".

(And again – if you realise you're doing and being any of this, don't be hard on yourself. You are in no way the only one, there are so many of us. It's how we've been taught to live – and there are so few role models to show us a different way. But now that you're understanding this in yourself, you can make change. In making change in yourself, not only do you come alive, but you can be such a role model, a lighthouse, to truly affect others on a fundamental level – and that's what the second half of this book is about. So hang in there.)

Stories and Security – Who Believes and Who Doesn't

We crave certainty and stability above all things – and yet we live in a time where the old certainties of external life have been shaken deeply, and people are left untethered, struggling to find security and belonging.

It's a very rare breed that actively seeks uncertainty. Even "adrenaline junkies" like those in extreme sports or high risk financial sectors – what they're ultimately seeking *is* certainty. They aren't seeking a lack of control, they are seeking the edge of control: they want to test their ability to securely manage a situation full of (what seems to us mortals) outrageously chaotic and insecure variables.

Certainty, stability and security, of a kind, can be found in the people we connect with. A tribe that believes the same as I do produces the comfort of, "You're okay, so I'm okay".

Phew.

And you can find a tribe that believes anything that appeals to you. Anything: from flat-earthers and doomsday preppers, to global political child abuse conspiracies and racist and religious terrorists, to those who believe in an extra-terrestrial reptilian ruling elite or that we're living in a computer simulation, The

Matrix style.

The chase for different means everything is relative, even agreed standards of what might be true. We live in a "post-Truth" world. Everything's up for grabs! As long as it brings the believer a sense of certainty, knowing, and belonging, it doesn't matter how kooky or inconsistent the belief is, only that "people like me" believe it too.

And anyone who believes different?

They become the enemy. These "Others" challenge the stories we tell about ourselves and the world around us which are our source of stability. Threaten my beliefs and you threaten my security... and so it becomes about for and against, who your tribe is and who they aren't – it's about who you stand with, and who you stand in opposition to.

Ironic, isn't it?

We chase the different and the new, but it can't be too different or new; it can't be too provocative to our stories. Comfort over challenge is not only preferred, it's actively sought after – even if challenge will ultimately enable and expand us, bringing us forward in life and creating more freedom with less struggle and more aliveness.

If you've ever been involved in any kind of personal

growth programme, you'll know the denial and turmoil that direct feedback about you can cause. It's the weirdest thing. The reflection is necessary for me to see blind spots and grow beyond limitation. I invite it, and yet part of me resists it. All my ego wants to hear is how wonderful I am, that I'm more than enough.

I've been doing this for a while, and it still takes a gulp before the leap. It still takes some serious openness and boldness for me to examine my closely held beliefs and stories.

But in the absence of this willingness to be so exposed and uncomfortable?

We stick our heads deeper into the sand. We double down on what we believe. We circle the wagons and close our minds. We attack before we get attacked. We lash out at the Others and anyone challenging our stories and upsetting our fragile certainty: "It's your fault I feel so disconnected, so dissatisfied, so frustrated!".

Part of it is to make us feel better, to feel right – but also in our endless chase for more, empty of knowing enough, the Others are the ones that will take from us. We need to get ours before they do, by whatever means necessary. There is no "for the common good" – it's pure childish ego grasping.

We are so in search of wanting to belong, and be okay, and be and have enough, we rarely examine the truth of our own beliefs, only who else is expressing them. We would rather blame and attack someone else for our feelings of discomfort and uncertainty than look within to find enough and yet make change to truly expand into more of life.

The result?

A small life indeed, and a scary, alienating, even hopeless, world when we consider those with different beliefs from us: "Who are these people? How can they believe that? Are they even human?!".

We are feeling powerless, insecure, scared, frustrated, anxious and angry. We just don't know what to do with the conflict, confusion and opposition in the world, sometimes just across the dining table, sometimes right between our own ears.

How to navigate all this?

We'll talk more later, but first, how about making your corner of the world a place you don't want to escape from, that you don't need to be afraid of? Instead of arguing and separating or hiding, how about connecting and building?

Being enough in yourself first is instrumental in your ability to make change, to make sure you're not part of the problem. It removes you from being rudderless in a world of constant change. It gives anchorage in true, unshakeable stability and belonging, so much deeper than shared belief and the approval of others or an empty "feel good" gained by gossip or social media trolling.

Know that in this age of extreme either/or black and white, it isn't the age of crossing barriers and seeking to understand or empathise. It might even be the age of "How far can you go?" where provocation wins over connection. Yet connection might be more required than ever before.

While seeking understanding, having empathy and being open may not be sexy – it's also hard. My own wife can be so very different and difficult to understand at times, let alone my neighbour or that idiot on the internet. Pointing the finger can be so much easier than connecting. Certainly easier, but rewarding? No.

So choose to play a much bigger game than petty separation and selfishness and "I need" and "I'm right, you're wrong". They are not the enemy. If anything, your old and limited beliefs are – your own feelings of emptiness and lack, fear and frustration, opposition and blame.

Be enough, have enough, yes – but don't settle for less and being limited in yourself. Go beyond the closed-minded judgements, the casual prejudice, the unconscious habits.

Nurture the constancy of your connection to your sense of Self. It's needed more than ever.

We're Afraid of Fear, We're Intense About Intensity

We don't like to be uncomfortable – *and* our Western culture reflects this back at us. It demonises any kind of intensity. Perfection has been deified in our cultural conditioning to such a degree that, for many of us, the merest sign of an elevated heart rate, of being uncertain, of feeling vulnerable, means we believe we're somehow doing it wrong.

The idea that life should be comfortable is a problem because it won't. Life will be intense and uncomfortable at times, but this doesn't mean you're doing it wrong. In fact, you're probably doing it right.

The problem with trying to find enough through comfort is that it involves holding any kind of intensity at arm's length. Growth, on the other hand, necessarily involves finding peace with uncertainty and change and feeling foolish and admitting that "I don't know".

If you think that any intensity looks like something you should avoid, that's a big problem. Achieving doesn't mesh with being totally in control, and that's the biggest problem: we're control freaks. Anything we can't control is seen as wrong.

The result? We over-medicalise and sedate and attempt to remove. We ignore inconvenient facts that run counter to our stories that provide a sense of security. We claim fake news and lose ourselves in conspiracy delusions and victimhood, all in an attempt to have intensity and uncomfortable truths about the world and ourselves be gone.

We say to kids, "Don't be afraid!" – teaching them from a young age that being afraid is wrong. So today, there are so many people who are in this wild feedback loop where they are afraid of being afraid, with panic attacks the result of this resistance to intensity and uncertainty.

But as the psychologist Jordan Peterson so beautifully says:

> *"You don't learn to not be afraid. You learn that you can cope and be brave. And those are way different things."*

The problem is we don't teach people to show up and learn to cope and be brave in the face of intensity or to be okay in the face of not being in control, of not knowing.

Which is a crime. In a world which will be unavoidably uncomfortable, uncertain, changing and risky, we have neutered ourselves. We have no means to deal with fear, challenge, and uncertainty head on. We as a culture would rather it just went away.

We would be better served by cultivating some skills to be able to choose to react to the circumstances of our life differently. Life will never be totally safe or secure. We can try our best to make it so, but our best to change and control can't cover it. An old Buddhist saying comes to mind: "It is easier to put on a pair of shoes than to wrap the earth in leather." Avoidance is never an answer, but making yourself competent in the face of fear, intensity, instability and uncertainty certainly is.

How do you make yourself more competent? How do you find the solution to what we've outlined in the above pages? That's what the next section is all about. This, for me, is always the best part: the way forward...

PART TWO: HOW TO BE

First, Decide

First, realise *you* get to decide what you want your life to be about. Decide you must, otherwise you're just unconsciously following everyone else – and you don't want to invest so much time and effort in pursuing something, only to realise you've been climbing the wrong mountain all along.

It's your life – you get to decide. So, what is it that you want? What is a successful life – *to you*?

Get very clear on what's truly important to you, what's nice to have, and what is simply detail and distraction: what are other people's urgencies and priorities.

In deciding, you may consider what Blaise Pascal, the 17th-century French philosopher, said many years ago: "All of humanity's problems stem from man's inability to sit quietly in a room alone."

Given the current mess of our mental health and seeming lack of genuinely thriving individuals, I say a big part of your definition of success should include simply being able to sit quietly, by yourself, alone in a room. To find fullness and satisfaction in each and every moment – and not automatically reach for your phone to be entertained, to try and fill it with the new and different. To sleep at night un-interrupted by worry and over-thinking. To not snap and be furious at the office printer or other inanimate object, traffic, or other people when they don't act like you want them to. To find peace in the middle of chaos. To give up insane expectations and perfectionism. To be able to balance wanting more with complete contentment with the way you are and the world is.

You have the freedom to decide how you want to live. You get to decide what success is – for you. Recognise that I'm not suggesting you give anything up. I'm suggesting an inner, spiritual path, but a true path – one that is whole, that embraces *all* of life. You don't need to give anything up, only rigid either/or thinking, limitation, emptiness, separation, and fear itself.

How? Here we go:

No More Donuts – Choose to Let Now Be Enough

To stop living the Donut Life, you need to know that enough is not caused, it is chosen – by you. Constantly seeking to find enough through our possessions, relationships, experiences, reputations and results does not bring us what we want. As author Ryan Holiday beautifully explains:

"We all think some external accomplishment is going to change everything, but it never seems to. It doesn't change how you see yourself, it doesn't change how you go through the world, it doesn't change what you feel like when you wake up in the morning...

You thought that doing important or impressive work will make you happy. This was precisely wrong. It's that being happy will help us do important and impressive work, quite possibly better and more pure work."

Instead of scrambling for more in the hope it will bring us to enough, secure satisfaction yourself. Choose it by claiming and knowing enough. Choose to let now *be* enough, a very useful phrase I stole from my esteemed colleague Narain Ishaya.

The bucket cannot be filled if it has a hole in it. Enough plugs that hole. It provides structure to the attaining and the appreciation of more. Without it, all the more in the world doesn't satisfy; it just pours out, leaving a soggy disappointment.

Enough is everything. Start by choosing enough – and yes, it's *that* simple: choose to let now be enough. Be present without expectations, demands and insistences. Stop wishing now was different, stop seeking to change or improve it. Now is not a mistake. Instead, be curious about what is here: eyes wide open, aware, alert and alive. Connect, have a direct relationship with reality, face to face.

I found this immensely tough in the beginning of my spiritual journey. I was taught how to choose to be filled with presence and Being, but at the same time I couldn't quite let it be enough. I had this incredibly pressing habit of impatience. I wanted it all yesterday. Maybe you're the same?

But it's not a virtue. The focus on wanting to be there already means we totally miss out on here.

You see, life is *not* a journey; it is this very moment that is right in front of you. This moment is life – everything else is a memory or a guess or a hope. Nice perhaps, but it's not real. It's a dream.

We lose life itself in the attempt to bring the future here quicker. Besides, impatience is a kind of fire that burns you up on the inside. It almost physically hurts. It makes you frustrated and lash out and you're no fun to be around. Nothing can ever be good enough.

Trust me, as a recovering impatience addict, learn to choose to be content. It is a powerful choice for aliveness, right now, regardless of what is happening in your life. Have passion, yes, but let it be a passion for more that finds it here; that doesn't throw away real life for a future maybe.

So show up to now, show up to life as it is. Don't let enough be caused by anything different. And when achievement and more comes through? What a bonus that is. When you have enough, when you are content, everything else is cherries on top.

Stop Doing, Embrace Non-Doing

"Practice non-action. Work without doing...
The sage does not attempt anything very big,
and thus achieves greatness."

— Lao Tzu, 6th-century Chinese philosopher and teacher

Ah, Lao Tzu and the Tao Te Ching. How many Westerners, such as myself, searching to regain our Zen moments and to fill the Donut life, came across Eastern spiritual texts such as this, and scrambled their Protestant work ethic, performance and more-oriented little minds?

In my search, I know I so puzzled over what I read about non-doing and undoing, such as the philosopher Alan Watts once wrote:

"A scholar tries to learn something everyday;
a student of Buddhism tries to
unlearn something daily."

How could I do or achieve anything without action? How could I have without chasing? How could I get better by forgetting? Being a product of the either/or thinking of peace or performance, I thought what was being taught was to give up. I therefore became a bit of a bum.

Rejecting money, working when I had to, being in the outdoors as much as I could, I gave up the pursuit of achieving and accolades and chose to chase happiness and satisfaction. You could say I rejected the outer game for the inner journey. I chose peace over performance. And I quickly became dissatisfied. A directionless, hedonistic anti-more lifestyle wasn't the answer either.

Like so many before me, I had mis-interpreted the teachings. I had little idea of how to Be, no matter what I was doing. Now I know better, I know the texts aren't talking about opposites. I know how to not do, and it has nothing to do with inaction.

Here's the thing: without action, nothing gets done. I'm not arguing with that. What I'm ultimately trying to sell to you is the *quality* of your action.

Quality involves realising work and motion is not always productive. Some work – such as what led to my swimming injury as a teen – is totally counter-productive. Quality work can only come from your Being; it is informed by your presence. Without Being, doing is empty.

Non-doing is the right term; it isn't *not*-doing. You see, in quality, presence-filled action, you don't do. You don't create. Your Being does.

This might be the hardest thing for us to get our heads around. To our way of thinking, if we stop doing, we stop creating. Peace becomes the opposite of performance and achieving – a passionless, dull place. But we've got it all wrong. Pure Being is the source of *all* creation, wisdom, passion and inspiration, not our small little doing minds.

Knowing this as a concept won't stop your ego from trying to claim credit though: "I'm a genius! I'm the greatest!". No, you're not. You were the vessel for greatness, not greatness itself. If you want to bring more greatness into the world? You have to get empty.

Empty?

It's what the Eastern (and the Western mystical) traditions espouse and what today's greatest performers in all fields have learnt to do. They practise over and over again so they can get out of their own way, and into the way of greatness. As Mark Divine, an ex-Navy SEAL, puts it: "Pure human potential comes not from within the mind, but from outside the mind, from the spirit."

Allowing Being to act is the core of mastery in any pursuit. Sure, there's learning skills and plans, tactics and information, but it all combines to create something special when you are not there, when you don't do a single thing.

So get empty. Empty yourself of ego. Empty yourself of pre-conceived ideas and expectations. Maybe have a sketch of a plan, a starting line or a story, but be willing to drop and run in an unplanned direction, to be innocent and not know, to hear the call of your intuition, and to meet the need of the moment.

Carry no shoulds, no doubts, no limits, no fear. Empty yourself and get receptive. This is how true creation comes to be.

It's simple but not easy, this being empty of everything, filled only with Being. It takes focus. It takes practise. Our habitual reliance on mental chatter and scattered thinking means this monkey mind of ours – an upset, irritated, irrational monkey at that – runs roughshod over our pure intuition and creative spark. Without focus the creative spark can never become a fire.

The doubt, the fear, "What will they think of me?", "What if I mess up?", the ego's concern with the end result and your reputation, all fill up your cup leaving no room for pure Being.

This is where the discipline to practise presence comes in. You have to detach from your monkey mind and your To-Do list and your ego and what you think you know. You have to be so familiar with Being, you become Being itself.

When the small you does nothing?

That is the source of all that is good. When you lose

yourself in Being, everything you do comes alive. You can meet the need of the moment, precisely. Zero struggle, just effortless, playful even. The small self disappears: "There is action, but no do-er", as Maharishi Krishnananda, my Bright Path Ishaya teacher put it. What's left is ideal. It's clarity, energy, creating, decisiveness, knowing. It's intuition, free of limitation, put to use.

Once again:

This is not about not working, but about letting work come through you. You don't create. Being does. You have to show up and align with it. You have to show up and be ready to work, but the quality of the work comes through Being.

Empty your cup, put Being first.

Don't Try to Become

Putting Being first means complete acceptance of yourself. It is pure alive authenticity. It is the end of the suffocating concern that "I am not enough", that paralysing self-doubt that creates so much exhausting anxiety, self-editing, self-evaluation, self-management and image control.

When you connect with your Being – your sense of presence and aliveness, the unchanging context to the forever shifting content of your life – doubt and insecurity disappear. You don't have to prove your existence, it is a fact. When you anchor yourself in your Self, there you are. Nothing to prove, nothing to hide. You are enough, simply in your Being, because you are alive.

Ahhh... here it's effortless to exist. It's so refreshing in comparison to constantly feeling like you need to be different to prove yourself worthy. How self-violent is that? Trying to find out what you need to be to others in order to feel accepted?

Man, I spent so much life trying to be acceptable, trying to fit in, trying not to offend, worried if I did. It's exhausting; it's the opposite of freedom. When I found some people who appeared to love me exactly as I was... what a relief to let go! Then I could begin to discover how to love myself too.

What I found was that the self-acceptance inherent in enough is key. However, much of the self-help and spiritual spheres, like the rest of capitalism and our culture, are based in the pursuit of more and different. Ranging from "Heal your hurts" to "Become somebody!" – the attitude is that you are not enough, *yet*; that you need to do something to become enough.

The message, "There's something wrong with you right now – you need to be different in order to be whole and happy" might not be explicit, but the resulting search is real. There are so many people trying to become better, trying to evolve, all with an underlying attitude of, "I shouldn't *be* like this", "I will be whole (and happy) when..." and carrying long lists of things about themselves that need fixing.

In my line of work I often find people searching for the exact same thing I was looking for. They tell me they're working on loving themselves – which is a beautiful thing to want to do. But they are making the same mistake I made.

We are so soaked in the zeitgeist of more, we have no way of seeing we are already enough. You, reading this, you too: your presence is rich, full, complete, whole. You need nothing here.

To experience this needing nothing, this source of having nothing to prove and nothing to hide, you just need to stop trying to change yourself. Stop judging yourself, and start Being.

In Being you find complete acceptance – and love. Love just happens, it just is; because to get here, full of Being, you can't carry your judgements of how you are lacking. Here, free of judgement, you already are love. You become the pre-existing source of love.

It's judgement and the belief that we need more to be done in order to become whole and enough that's our problem. And, as we've learnt, if you seek more it will always be found.

As the psychoanalyst Carl Jung once said, "We cannot change anything unless we accept it. Condemnation does not liberate, it oppresses". It doesn't feel like condemnation, but the myopic focus on becoming and being different absolutely is. We're trying to be someone we're not, someone we think we should be. And that may be the most self-violent thing we can do.

I initially swapped one kind of self-management and image control for another, more spiritual kind – and that's what we all invariably do when we get on an inner path. It's still prison, just a more noble kind of prison.

So set yourself free. Truly help yourself by getting rid of the goal of transformation. Stop trying to attain and become. You don't have to change.

And yet, yes, it's a wonderful thing to become different! To transform, to be better. But it can't be done through effort or a focus on your broken-ness. Paradoxical huh? When you look for a way out of the madness of the Donut Life, of wanting to find a foundation of enough, you want to change. But you bring your very problem of more before enough, of doing before Being, of different before contentment with you.

Leave it at the door.

A genuine inner path of self-help is about being the source of enough. It is a practice of being content with the way things are, with who you are too. And it's the weirdest thing. You do get, you do become, your sharp edges do drop off. But that is only through the total self-acceptance of you, the acceptance of the moment. Through not seeking to change, the natural, vibrant and alive version of you can come about... and not the version you think you should be.

At its purest, finding enough is not a path of creativity – it's a path of being receptive to what is. It's a path of letting go, not adding anything to yourself. There is so much stuff in spirituality about affirmations and manifestations and creating your reality – but all of it is doing.

Doing is a strong habit. I was forever asking my teacher, Maharishi (cue whiny voice), "But tell me: what else do I have to *do*?". The answer was always nothing; just fully and completely choose to Be – yet as simple as that instruction is, it was the hardest thing in the world for me to follow for a long time.

So let me repeat: your problem is doing. You need to wean yourself off the addiction to it in order to step into Being. Don't do on your spiritual path; this is not the place.

You don't need more. This moment doesn't need more. By letting go of the need for different, you can be completely absorbed in what is in front of you. All Flow states, peak experiences, Zen moments – they are all characterised by a complete immersion in the moment. You can't be enraptured in the now *and* think it needs improving.

We all have a belief that we are not enough, we are wrong, we are lacking. But it is in belief only, not reality. While we have made plenty of mistakes, we are not wrong. Not in our Beings. You are enough. And you will become more. But right here right now, stop looking and evaluating and criticising yourself. Stop carrying your mistakes. Stop seeing them as proof you are wrong. Just Be.

Align with the perfection of your already existing presence. Accept your past hurts, all the shame and regret and guilt and powerlessness. It sucked, but it can't unhappen, it won't change. You however, in acceptance, will.

Your practice is to approach this perfect acceptance of now time and time again. It means you wear out the addiction and habits of thinking you are not enough and you need to become. All of your sharp bits are there because of fear and the control fear causes. When you enter into enough, you free yourself of fear. You step in and realise that you can let go now, and life is simple, easy, full. Your choice is rewarded.

You realise that by letting go now, the future turns out all right – in fact, *better* than you could even imagine. Through the surrender to what is, to what is right in front of you and what is within you, by stopping trying to force life to happen a particular way so you can have enough, you can start truly showing up to life. Then you can start working *with* life, and not against it.

Surrender and Control

"The Master doesn't seek fulfilment.
Not seeking, not expecting, he is present, and can welcome all things."

— Lao Tzu

This will take trust! Yes it will. Letting go into Being is surrendering control over life's twists and turns – and we love control. We have a belief that control is power. But as Byron Katie, a prominent self-help teacher, says: "If you want real control, drop the illusion of control. Let life live you. It does anyway."

Surrender is seeing clearly and completely embracing – by offering no resistance to – the reality of the present moment. We, however, tend to be very poor at this. We live in a world of plans and expectations, frustrations and shoulds, impatience and wanting to be there already. Rarely do we experience now directly – pure, free of mental judgement and prejudice.

How can we play the game of life when we're so busy wishing the game was different?

We can't.

Friedrich Nietzsche taught a concept of Amor Fati (loving one's fate) that is popular at the moment. Amor

Fati can only be experienced by surrendering to the facts of now, and thus avoiding the stories of suffering: "If only...", "I could/should have...", "If it wasn't for...".

Nietzsche writes:

> *"My formula for greatness in a human being is Amor Fati: that one wants nothing to be different, not forward, not backward, not in all eternity. Not merely bear what is necessary, still less conceal it... but love it."*

The only time you stop enjoying being where you are is when you think you should be somewhere you're not. Reality is not different or change or more. It is not the past or future. It is absolute acceptance and communion with the truth of what is right in front of you and right within you. Living Amor Fati is letting now be enough so fully you *love* what is.

So: stop wishing, stop resisting. Get here and get clear. Then, and only then, can you truly do something with what you find.

The Courage to Do

"Give me the serenity to accept the things I cannot change,

The courage to change the things I can,

And the wisdom to know the difference."

— Serenity prayer of the Alcoholics Anonymous

While many military, athletic and business Do-ers might associate surrender with negative connotations of giving up or becoming a push-over, surrender is anything but weak.

Surrender into Being gives you wisdom. It gives you the ability to clearly see where you're getting in your own way. Not only do you see where you're pushing so hard and yet have no control, you see where you don't have the courage to create the change you can.

We are so impatient. We push for action when there is nothing to be done, where the only answer is to wait and see. And we're timid too. We sit on things we want to do for far too long, trying to make the course of action more comfortable by postponing. Of course, this never works.

Surrender – and your resulting clarity and wisdom – shakes your tree so everything that is rotten falls out. All the stories, the compromises, the imbalances increasingly fall on the ground in front of you, becoming more and more obvious and harder and harder to live with.

When you see you've been sitting on the fence, the realisation means it gets sharper and more pressing against delicate areas. You can't avoid anymore. You can't ignore. You can't pretend. Surrender means an inner urge to not compromise life gets stronger and stronger – thus any compromise just gets more and more uncomfortable.

It's actually quite a shock to some people – in a spiritual path they were looking for a kind of peaceful sedation, to make their problems go away. But what they got was a heart and soul kick start: a defibrillator straight to the spirit.

I was more than a little shocked when I started to see how much compromise was in my life, because I told myself there wasn't much. Amazing how asleep we can be until we're woken, huh? Temporarily uncomfortable it may have been, but I'm glad for it. It meant I could live a much fuller, more alive life, and that's worth everything to me.

So surrender is not giving up, no – it's becoming more authentic and bold in the best possible sense.

There is No Path

"'This is my way; where is yours?' – Thus I answered those who asked me 'the way'. For the way – that does not exist."

— Friedrich Nietzsche

The mad rush to do and achieve more means we give little to no time and space for surrender to our own clarity. There's little chance to gain a sense of what is truly right for us. We end up blindly following someone else's definition of success – and it's a big part of why we are so dissatisfied, unhappy and frustrated, insecure and anxious. We're trying to fulfil someone else's standards, we're trying to live someone else's life.

We're looking for *the* path – but it doesn't exist, it never has. As mythologist Joseph Campbell wrote:

"If you can see your path laid out in front of you step by step, you know it's not your path. Your own path you make with every step you take. That's why it's your path."

Through surrender to the wisdom of Being and by ending compromise, you will be shown your path. And it feels right. Only this can give true satisfaction and fulfilment. Nourished by your whole Being, you can't go wrong by walking your path.

But why do so few actually do this? Sometimes it seems to come down to caring about what other people think.

In the Donut Life, we depend on others for approval, for belonging. Our shared beliefs and stories offer us a feeling of certainty and security in the face of a world that is constantly changing. We become followers. We fear doing things differently, we fear being wrong and suffering rejection.

To branch out on our own? To throw away the received path of the tribe, the comfort of feeling like we are a part of something? Hooo... that can take boldness, especially in the beginning.

But if you want to be truly alive, is there any other way?

How terrified was I when I decided to merely stick my toe in the water of being an Ishaya monk by doing a six month retreat? Crying terrified. And yet I was laughing at the same time. Terrified and overjoyed. Hmmmm... in the middle of this mess of tears and snot and giggles, I had enough clarity to see the fear of my ego of doing something different from everyone else, and the love of my heart from finally being on my right path.

And you know which one appealed the most.

By putting presence first, you find the only certainty in the whole universe. Your Being is a fact. It's the one thing you can truly rely on. It doesn't depend on what's happening in the world, what you believe or who shares your vision. It never changes, no one can take it away from you. It's who You are.

With this internal anchor, no chaos, change or uncertainty is threatening. None of it. You become certainty itself. You can navigate all challenge and change when you align with the constancy of your Self.

Presence is the end of fear. When you lose Being, it appears again: fear, loss, comparison, wrong, not enough, being rejected. Head to presence and Being first.

You start to see fearful and judgmental beliefs, stories and habits a mile away. In the absolute clarity of your Being, you'll *feel* them as restriction, a weird dislocation from reality. This awareness means it's a simple thing to stop feeding them. With no nourishment, they lose momentum and die. You didn't do anything – you stopped, and expanded into more rightness because of it.

Within we find the belonging we have craved. The clawing need for approval and recognition dies. The self-doubt and editing and constrictive comparison goes too. With nothing to prove and nothing to hide, you are set free.

You won't get stuck in tribalism, in us versus them. You

don't need to attack or defend. You don't need to lash out to make yourself feel better. You'll find debating a belief so tedious.

You give up the insane "me and mine first" selfish grab for more where others are the competition. You can truly understand, connect, build, lift up, and share to all. You have enough, you are enough. You don't lack, you aren't empty, you have more than enough to give.

You can enjoy the feeling of being part of something bigger than you, but you're not imprisoned by it. You enjoy your people, but you're not dependent, you're not defined or constrained by them.

You are free to align with something far more powerful and fulfilling to you than fear, uncertainty, and "what they think". As Osho, the spiritual teacher, says:

"Only disciplined people become free, but their discipline is not obedience to others: their discipline is obedience to their own voice. And they are ready to risk anything for it."

Discipline and the Dance

Being filled with enough means you need nothing.

Again: this does not mean you do nothing. You *need* nothing, which is wonderful – there's no stick, no addiction, no emptiness. But you still *want* to do. You are still creative. More so, because you're truly aligned with the source of inspiration. When you surrender to your voice and your right path, you'll be so fired up you'll have no problems finding things to do.

Discipline is required to get things done; without it nothing happens. As Lao Tzu wrote, a journey of a thousand miles begins with a single step – but a single step is not enough. You need the commitment to be consistent to finish the journey. Without discipline you get nowhere.

Now, discipline needs a direction, a goal in mind. It needs a top of the mountain to climb. You want to know what your definition of success is, you want to know where you're aiming... but then crucially, you must break it all down into what you can do today.

But we rarely do this. Everywhere in life we focus so much on the end result, on the more we want, we forget the single step in front of us. The top of the mountain is such a long way off and so intimidating we often talk ourselves out of even starting. We procrastinate and "get ready" but never get going. And besides, if we ever finally go, we're so busy looking up at the end it's so easy to trip and fall flat on our faces on the smallest stone that's right in front of us.

I've had many flashes of insight, these beautiful, exciting ideas... and so few of them got off the ground because I never stopped planning how they would unfold. You can't plan everything, often life shows you the path as you walk it. All you need is a beginning, all you need is now.

This small step, here now? Do-able, so do-able. The future? Impossible. Our poor little minds freak out.

Krishna taught this precise lesson in the Bhagavad Gita, thousands and thousands of years ago:

> *"You have the right to work, but for the work's sake only. You have no right to the fruits of work. Desire for the fruits of work must never be your motive in working. Never give way to laziness, either...*
>
> *Be even-tempered in success and failure: for it is this evenness of temper which is meant by yoga. Work done with anxiety about results is far inferior to work done without such anxiety, in the calm of self-surrender. Seek refuge in the knowledge of Brahma* [Being, your higher Self]. *They who work selfishly for results are miserable."*

We thought Krishna and other spiritual masters were saying renounce the rewards, the fruits of work, but no. They're saying: give up the *attachment* to the rewards. And don't be lazy, either! Do, act, but let the results come and go. You're not truly in control of external success or failure, you're only in control of enough. Let work be the reward. Put Being first. Want but don't need. Don't work to get, because then you will not perform to the best of your abilities, and you will be miserable.

Sportspeople have known forever how the fixation on the end result brings poor performance. Andre Agassi, the tennis player, wrote about being free from thoughts of winning:

> *"I instantly play better. I stop thinking, start feeling. My shots become a half-second quicker, my decisions become the product of instinct rather than logic."*

Quality only comes from what you can do now, regardless of how horrible and unfair – or even how amazing – just a moment ago was.

So – break it all down. Pave your pursuit of more with single steps of now. Don't focus on the goal, forget success, forget failure, forget what just happened. Stop trying to prove yourself to be enough. Be enough, and know you will get better through your single steps.

Here you are free of all overwhelm, overload, fear, stress, struggle. All of it. Everything becomes playful and curious, instinctual and inspired... the opposite of heavy and needy, over-thought and forced. The pressure vanishes and the dance begins. When you need nothing, you are able to be so graceful – dancing without a single care for a misstep, without trying to get there to the end of the song. Here, through a gentle discipline to the dance of Being, quality, Flow and joy can reveal themselves.

BRINGING IT ALL TOGETHER

How to Make a Difference

So, a bunch of things to consider and to Be, all in the name of living a whole, balanced and truly alive life.

Prioritising presence, finding a foundation in Being and enough, chasing more through want not need – everything we've been talking about makes a real and complete difference in your life. I've seen it in myself, I've seen it in so many others, time and time again. It's well worth investing in.

The good news is that by helping yourself first, you also help your loved ones, your community, the world too.

And it's sorely needed.

So many people searching. So many people lost, angry, uncertain and scared. "What can we rely on? How do we navigate? How can we help our kids and loved ones, our neighbourhood?".

There is so much finger pointing, so much attack, so much separation and difference. So many looking to the external world, blaming or seeking to change this person and that system, slamming or promoting this politics or that lifestyle.

There is so much missing in the middle of all this – working from the Donut Life perspective will *always* be limited. At worst, it means it's your fault I'm so frustrated and don't feel like I am enough. You are the cause of my problems; to end my problems you must change or be controlled. I don't have enough, my life is continually lacking. I need so much more – and I fear you will take from me. Attack and defend, grab and hold, separate and blame.

At best, the Donut Life perspective requires the outside world to be different so that *then* I will find ease, contentment, fulfilment and peace. I *need* more to get enough; what I want is caused. But need is always limited and hollow – even with the most wonderful of intentions.

Ervin Seale, a self-help teacher, describes the problem beautifully, and what to do about it:

"Overconcern for a suffering world is often a projection of one's own need. And many a needy one has helped himself by helping others. Some have become ineffectual nuisances because they did not realize that the main business of living is individual growth, the seeking of the kingdom of heaven which is within...

Of all the people I know who are serving society, those who are making the greatest contributions in alleviating human ills and wants are those who have themselves in hand."

Get yourself in hand first.

It's important. As a young student when learning of injustice or horrible news, I wanted to *do* something to help. I began by pointing the finger and yelling. "You're wrong! It's your fault! You must change!". In the beginning it was great, doing something felt empowering.

And you know what happened? The more I shouted and the more angry I got, the more walls I found. People would close down in the face of my onslaught. People rarely change through shame or belittling. They just dig in deeper.

I realised it's very difficult to change someone else. They tend to resent it. Me? That's one person I can change – actually, the *only* person.

It makes a difference.

Outer confusion and conflict stem very much from inner confusion and conflict. End opposition and conflict, emptiness and uncertainty, anger and fear within yourself, and you end it in your interactions with others. Balance and reconcile the extremes, overcome the separation and the limitation within yourself. End lack and need, find more than enough, be solid and stable. Make the inner work a priority and you won't lash out at others, nor will you add to the chaos, even unconsciously. You'll be able to truly give and not take.

As Phil McGraw, the TV psychologist wrote, “Anger is nothing more than an outward expression of hurt, fear and frustration”. If we’re honest and brave enough, we can see why we get angry: the unfairness, the pain, the outrage, the fear of losing something, the feeling of being impotent, of not being enough. That’s exactly why I was shouting. “We ache for the gap between the world as it is, and the world as it should be”, as author Jamie Wheal puts it.

But don’t just ache, create.

If we come to understand the hurt, fear, and frustration in ourselves, we can learn to understand it in others. If we start with understanding, we can stop attacking and instead connect – which wins every time over blame and belittling.

So – can you give connection and empathy through understanding what it’s like to be afraid, to be confused, even messed up, to be blinded by belonging or clinging to certainty through belief? It doesn’t mean you condone someone’s beliefs or actions, but it certainly means you can show them a better, more expansive way, free of fear.

It won’t be easy, but it will be rewarding. It will give you more of life, in all ways.

Do the right thing. Let Being inform the integrity of anything you might do or say. Your connection with

Being not only creates connection with quality and truth, it creates connection with others. As author Maya Angelou beautifully wrote:

> *"People will forget what you said, people will forget what you did, but people will never forget how you made them feel."*

At the very least, you might want to realise that change is a long process, and anger will kill you if you let it fester. If you want to make a difference, you have to be in for the long haul. Keeping your sense of humour and perspective is crucial. Stay filled with peace and presence, alive to what is actually here. No matter what you think should be – regardless of how strongly you feel – focus on and live from what you actually have: otherwise you're living in need and a future when.

Patience and contentment, free of frustration, are needed for the journey of any kind of becoming – in yourself and in the world. Don't wait for anything to give you the life you think you want. Find calm, clarity and certainty within your Self first of all.

Spiritual masters have been telling us this forever – to master suffering and find true fulfilment is not so much about creating a different world, a more padded delusion. What is truly valuable, to all of us, is knowing certainty, contentment, and enough. It's the appreciation of the beauty, stability and practical usefulness of each of our own Beings, as they are, here and now – not later when the world or our lives have changed or become more.

Find your way *and* help out. Be, as Gandhi exhorted, the change you wish to see in your world: two birds, one stone. Prioritise going beyond imbalance, limitation, need and suffering. Find the platform to truly make a difference, free of fear and frustration – find right action guided by your right inner voice.

This is an inner journey. Change starts with you.

You Are Not Just One Person

"But what can I do?", you may ask... "I'm only one person. Being the change is not enough". Yet Jesus, Buddha, Lao Tzu, Krishna, Mary... they were only one person too, and all of them are still known today – and not so much for what they did, but for what they discovered inside themselves.

Think about it. No matter what you like or dislike about the belief structures that have sprung up around these individuals, we still know their names, thousands of years later. We still tell ourselves stories about them, we use them to guide and orient us, even if we think we don't.

We disagree on what they said or what they did, but we have little doubt on how they make us feel. The presence of their Beings, their lived example, still speaks to us. You can have such an impact too.

Unshakeable, deep, clear Being and presence... it's powerful, far more powerful than we can imagine from the sole perspective of doing more. As this passage from the Hua Hu Ching, an ancient Taoist text, describes:

"Do you imagine the universe is agitated? Go into the desert at night and look out at the stars. This practice should answer the question.

The superior person settles her mind as the universe settles the stars in the sky. By connecting her mind with the subtle origin, she calms it. Once calmed, it naturally expands, and ultimately her mind becomes as vast and immeasurable as the night sky."

Not losing your head like so many around you, not small and petty, not limited and lacking, not chaotic and uncertain – wide open, still, calm, clear, wise, loving, compassionate and powerful. Only in the depths of presence does your mind become truly useful, and to all.

The fact is you're having an impact anyway. You are. Consider your loved ones. As author James Baldwin wrote about our kids:

"Children have never been very good at listening to their elders, but they have never failed to imitate them."

I knew my kids didn't listen. What shocked me was when I became aware that they didn't miss a single thing. The fact is, they're not the only ones watching. So many people are searching – even unconsciously – for what to do, who to Be. They're looking for clues, for what's "right", for someone to follow.

Show them something truly valuable.

Be a source of stability, comfort and inspiration. Reassure and accept all with your presence. Be enough, and then others can also drop any pretence and attempts to be different; who they are not. Let your example shine. Let it be an invitation for them to find enough too, exactly as they are. Show them that it's okay to have ideas of more, to have passion and make change, but base it in the pure joy and satisfaction found in the contentment with the way things are.

Why not bring your Being forward and intentionally make your life something clarifying and stabilising, something truly valuable and useful, something lasting? Why not aim high, at mastery? Why not aim to live an example that will speak throughout the ages?

What else are you going to do?

Some Things You Can Do to Prioritise Being

Even though much of this book has talked about Being, there is much you can do. In fact, in order to create a new habit, even one of Being, you must intentionally do something different; and repeatedly. It is only the application of something, time and time again, that means you can embody it. So, don't just read this book – discipline yourself to Being. Commit to an inner journey to prioritise presence.

It can't be a case of wishful thinking. Rare as hen's teeth are those who can simply will themselves into remembering Being all the time. You'll need to make change – enjoyable and rewarding change – but change nonetheless.

The habits of the endless need for more, limitation and negativity, getting into our heads and worrying and regretting, of struggling and stressing are strong. We've fed them for so long, they have some momentum. They are culturally supported too, in so many ways: by the people around us, by the messages we get from media, by the very cultural programming we pick up from an early age that is deep in our bones.

These words can remind you to be filled with presence, to let now be enough. Remembering is good for now, but repetition and reapplication means you stop feeding the habits of forgetting forever.

So – here's a few things you can practically do:

1). Prioritise Presence

Take the time to work out what you want from life. Get clear on what success is, for you, and recalibrate this often. Detail the external stuff that you want to achieve and experience, yes, but also – and most importantly – define the inner nature of success for yourself.

We've explored various ideas in this book: Being, presence, the Self, quality, rightness, peace, contentment... but how would *you* define that? Is it love? Aliveness? Freedom? Ease? Zero suffering? Nothing to prove, nothing to regret, nothing to fear?

When you start to get a handle on what the inner nature of success is, how will you remind yourself of it? How will you keep it alive, not letting it be forgotten, slipping away into the busy-ness of your day? How will you stay inspired and on track?

Here's what I suggest:

We all create To-Do lists. The degree of action on those lists varies, but they are a very useful thing. Planning and prioritising, breaking down your goals to small steps, is necessary in life. If you were driving somewhere, you'd plan your route. Or trust the Sat-Nav, but you wouldn't just aimlessly drive out your gate – unless you wanted an uncertain outcome, an adventure.

(And adventure certainly has its part in life: you want to balance planning with spontaneity, discipline with goofing off. But as we've also said, these things aren't opposites, they aren't either/or. Planning is not the opposite of adventure – in fact, if you do it right, planning sets a framework for more adventure, not less.)

I suggest that every morning, before you plan your day and what you want to do, reflect on how you want to do it. In other words, write a To-Be list.

In writing this list, you're reminding and inspiring yourself in terms of how you want to show up today, of what's truly important to you, of presence and Being and how you want it to be the foundation of everything that you do. You're setting a higher standard, holding yourself to something much more than an empty chase for material more.

You can even ask yourself, given the challenges that you can predict will happen to you today – and we all know what they might be on a given day if we take the time to consider them – how you want to Be in the face of it all. So when it hits – and it's never a case of "if", only when – you're ready, you've planned, you know how you'd like to respond to the unwelcome and unwanted.

Rather than just crashing through life and looking back with a slap on your forehead and feelings of regret, guilt, shame or wasted time, you're intentionally planning presence.

You're not just heading out the gate and hoping for the best. You're prioritising Being, purposely placing the quality of your Self first – all so you can fully live life the way you want to, rather than letting life live you, dragging you around by the scruff of the neck.

2). Practise Being

You get steadfast in Being through practise; you develop the choice muscle to let now be enough by persistence and repetition. A practice cuts through limitation, negativity and imbalance. It brings forward rightness, wisdom and quality. It means you forget to forget. It means you stop thinking you're not enough, that you can't have more.

What kind of practice?

Rumi once wrote, "Let the beauty we love be what we do, there are hundreds of ways to kneel and kiss the ground". There are hundreds of practices that nicely disconnect you from need and the unceasing chase for

"What's next?", that align you with the contentment and wisdom of Being. I practise the Bright Path Ishayas' Ascension meditation – you may prefer yoga or Tai Chi or journalling or mindful walking or sitting with a coffee sans phone, doing nothing.

There are better and worse ways for sure, but who am I to tell you your right path?

Pick one!

Find something that's simple and that allows you to go beyond the worries and concerns, the frantic busy-ness, need and fear of your mind. Choose a means to fill up with presence. Get a way to step back from the washing machine of life – so you can see it all spinning around from outside the glass, and not be tumbled around in it.

A different habit is key to ending the Donut Life. Practise non-doing consistently, and yet effortlessly. Just do it – make the choice for Being diligently until it is second nature, until you realise it as your true nature.

3). Do What You Love, More

Doing what I loved showed me how full and rich life could be; it showed me potential. It showed me what life was like when I forgot the endless striving for more. Enthralled by the moment, free from regret and need and worry and self-management, I could settle deep in the fulfilment of enough.

Maybe you remember moments like these in your life, the absolute completeness and satisfaction? They were perfect. There was nothing missing, we wouldn't change a thing.

There's also an undeniable quality and power that comes from following your sense of what you love. It really is a sign post to your right purpose in life, to how you might bring as much meaning as possible to your time here on Earth.

These times are so valuable to us as an indicator of what it's like to truly be alive – the possibility of our lives. So get going on that. Do more of what you love, it's important.

Now, many of you might still be saying at this point, "But Arjuna, my life is different from yours. You're a lazy, lay-about monk. You don't understand what I have going on, what I want to achieve. I've got things to do – and besides, my work is my one, true love".

But what if I do understand, completely?

The great Do-ers of the world, with your awesome drive and Type-A personalities, have an extremely hard time not working. And yet Steven Kotler, the Flow state author and researcher, has shown that more highly creative ego-free non-doing productivity comes when you regularly set aside time to do things that you love. And it sets your life on fire!

This is mind-blowing – and guilt causing – to you great Do-ers, but what if more could be easy? Here's my challenge to you. If you're dedicated enough to work 100 hour weeks, are you dedicated enough to truly become better, in every part of life?

Maybe you can be willing to set aside time for balance, time for more love and joy – as an experiment. There's nothing to lose beyond your addiction to pushing and grinding, and you can always go back to the old ways should the guilt get too much for you – right?

4). Ah, But Also Love What You Do

Okay – however, as perfect a guide as love is, let's add a proviso. I'm writing these words about balance because once I was wildly imbalanced, forever chasing more of what I loved with no ability to choose to love everything I did.

I began this inner journey because I wanted no ordinary moments – none. I wanted an end to suffering, worry and fear. But I think more crucially, I wanted an end to boredom, to "ho-hum" and tediousness. Again, I think this is important to state: we do a great many things from a state of "should". Choosing to stop doing mind-numbing, soul compromising tasks just because "I have to" is powerful.

Love can be caused and created, yes; but what very few people know is love is also a choice, an attitude. Like we've talked about, the important thing in life is not so much what we do, but how we do it.

Our approach is everything – so realise that boredom is a choice. Our minds are such that we can make anything tedious: anything and everything. Learn to choose differently.

Be aware of your attitude and internal dialogue to any given situation or person. Shake it up. Claim the power of definition for yourself; don't let events and people define you.

Appreciation and gratitude will show you the way, they are a very slippery slope to love – and as such they are choices well worth cultivating into habits. No wonder gratitude journals and meditations are everywhere. Write, speak, do – and most importantly – Be appreciation and gratitude.

Make the most of your choice. Do what you love – but perhaps most importantly, love everything you do.

5). Let the Opposite of Love Be Your Wake-up Call

Let the presence of struggle, overwhelm and negativity in your life be a wake-up call. Make it an alarm bell that simply means you're out of alignment with the source of quality and rightness; that you're focusing on the wrong things.

Regardless of how much you have to do or how ambitious your goals may be, let overwhelm and stress be a reminder that you have unplugged from your power socket – and you are useless without that presence.

What do you have to do?

The problem is that you forgot, so the answer is simply to remember. Come back to Being. Re-prioritise presence. Completely. Stop being in the future, stop thinking about everything you have to do, stop listening to fear and doubt. Return to calm, clear presence and what is right in front of you.

If it's happening a lot, if life is getting sticky, often? You will have stopped or seriously reduced your inner practises. Re-commit.

Also be aware of your resistance, control and shoulds, as in, "This should not be happening to me!". The fact is it *is* happening. Step back, get clear. Surrender to what is; fully accept what you cannot control, make the most of what you can.

If you're finding yourself judgemental of others, wanting to attack or defend? You've left the security of your own Being. Be certain in your Self again. Go beyond your stories and beliefs, anchor yourself deep within presence.

Recognise that being triggered by someone can show you so much. Make it all about you. You may have words with this person, you may not, but first love them exactly as they are. Don't seek to change them. Then see if you really need to speak or not – but choose to connect rather than divide, build rather than destroy.

6). Give, More

I hate to call it a hack, but perhaps it is. What is this little trick that means you can quickly find enough?

Give. Give more.

The only reason we don't give more is because we're insecure, afraid we don't have enough. We feel we don't have enough money or time or energy... and of course, being good people, we'd like to give and we plan to give – but in the Donut Life, it's always a case of "*When* I get more, *then*...". You never find enough this way, you have to start giving regardless.

The cool thing about giving is that it shows you that you have enough to give. It takes your focus away from lack, and gives you the direct opposite. As the famous basketball coach John Wooden wrote,

> *"Three of the things we want most – happiness, freedom, and peace of mind – are always attained when we give them to others. Give it away to get it back."*

So just start. Give – anything, everything; you can't lose. Have a generosity of spirit. See where you can be of service to others. That may be money or goods, it may be a smile, an ear, or a shoulder. But perhaps more importantly, as we've been talking about throughout this book, start with yourself.

Give yourself a break. Come to terms with the necessity of making mistakes to learn and grow. Give others the freedom to grow through experience too. Even if you want to be a great role model, leader, mentor or parent, don't try and appear perfect. Being honest about your mistakes is the greatest thing you can do to free not only yourself, but everyone around you. Honesty and creativity, open and compassionate connections... something really dynamic and powerful is created when mistakes aren't vilified. When perfection is the aim, everyone becomes rigid, fearful, separate; they disclose and risk nothing. Creating positive and growthful relationships takes great humility and openness on your behalf. Give that too.

Give a wonderful example. Walk your talk. Your

presence speaks far louder than your words and deeds, so put that first. Be balanced, chase more *and* find enough: be open and unconditionally loving and yet hold high standards.

Give authenticity. Don't try and be someone you're not. Be enough as you are, align with your right path, be courageous in following it.

Give what you want to receive. Maybe that's understanding, patience, love, empathy, maybe that's looking after people, if you want to be looked after. But perhaps also – when asked for – an honest and truthful opinion. That's valuable; and rare too.

Give inclusion. Give to all of those around you, don't make life about what "I can get for myself and mine". It will never make sense to your ego, but your whole life will transform.

As Martin Luther King, Jr. said, in order to be of true service, "You only need a heart full of grace, a soul generated by love". Give and you get that back, and so much more.

7). Don't Settle for Less

Part of waking up and making the most of life is that we stop pointing the finger; we stop blaming everyone else, we stop waiting for the world to change so we can be happy and fulfilled. We stop believing that stress and struggle is necessary to get things done, that anxiety and depression are an inevitable fact of the human condition, that we have to choose a life of either more or enough.

So, I say, wake up. Stop doing these things. Stop settling for less in yourself.

See where you believe in the normality of suffering. See limitation and fear, see where you worry incessantly, judge yourself harshly or simply give up. See where you're afraid of what others will think. See where you attack or defend, where you blame or react wildly, where you withhold love or empathy.

I realise this can be uncomfortable, but it's necessary. Welcome it. This is your path to truly being more. Awareness is half the battle, so well done.

You don't have to do anything with what you find, just stop feeding it. Come into the complete presence of your Being. Aligned in this fullness of enough, with nothing to prove and nothing to hide, go for whatever more your heart says is right. From here, choose to say and do different things.

Seek wholeness, balance, aliveness. Build a life you don't need to regularly escape from. Create a world that you're not afraid of, one that you love. Find a relationship with your Self that makes your full potential possible. Don't compromise, stop settling for less.

The Finger Points Back at Your Own Heart

So – hopefully I've shown you the importance of balancing your pursuit of more with finding enough. That it's not about hiding from the world, but it's about finding quality of action, where everything you do and say and are is informed by presence and Being. That in Being you need nothing, and the world becomes your playground.

Hopefully I've conveyed the beauty and the power of non-doing, that for millennia certain spiritual masters have pointed the finger towards as a profoundly useful and fulfilling way to live life, free of regret and compromise, stress and uncertainty, conflict and fear.

Hopefully I've shown you that you were never broken or lacking. You may have made mistakes – we all have – but You were never wrong. You never could be, you never can be, for you always are. Your Being needs nothing. You are enough, always. You are whole and complete, always. And with this foundation, there can be forever more.

Hopefully I've shown you that your loved ones copy you. They won't listen to what you tell them, but they won't fail to use your example as guidance. Give them an example that is truly valuable. Find fulfilment and the true anchor within, operate from clarity not instability, work from want and excitement not need and lack. Show them what it's like to truly be alive.

At the very least, I hope I've given you something to think about. Perhaps that hustle, control, judgement, worry, frustration and anger isn't actually helping you get the results you want. And that might encourage you to trust and let go and do less more often, filling your moments instead with Being and the completeness you find there.

I know this has been the way for me. I even took vows as a monk, so much was I wanting to explore Being more and more deeply. But, by golly, there was a ton of trust in the beginning.

The trouble with this whole approach of Being is finding someone who knows what they're talking about. It's so easy to misunderstand the teachings – I know I did, a thousand times.

While a guide is a mighty fine and even necessary idea, the true teacher is your own Being. Have role models for sure, but if they're any good they will ultimately point the finger back at your own heart. And we need that external reminder, because it is remarkably hard – maybe impossible – for the ego to trust your Self.

Having no protocol is terrifying for all of us growing up rote learning objective facts and theories. The experts say, "Do this and you will find success"; they pronounce, “This is the truth” – and we listen. Having to become your own expert on your own path is extremely unsettling. “What if I’m wrong?”, “What if they laugh at me?”. For someone so used to finding and remembering the right answer in order to get a good grade in school, having no external right answer is... threatening.

Yet I can testify that trust, surrender, non-doing comes through. The embracing of enough really works, and continues to do so for me. The only times things have gotten sticky is when the little self, the ego, has tried to control it. When I’ve been focused on protecting my reputation, proving myself, wanting to be right. When I’ve given into fear and doubt and I haven’t headed for the peace and the certainty of my Being. When I’ve stuck with my past plan rather than sensing – or even asking – what is needed now.

You can trust surrendering to Being – I know that – but you want to know it too.

Again – you want a practice. You want a path, techniques and tools, regular rituals of prioritising presence and being enough. The force of personal and cultural history is too great otherwise. You need to have useful boundaries and a gentle discipline; otherwise, your mind, your body, your family and friends, your culture pull you back into struggle and control and “I’ll be happy when...”.

So, commitment, discipline, and consistency are extremely useful. You have to show up. But show up to now, to presence, fresh, open, free of expectations and insistences and demands. Come clean, with no resistances and shoulds and plans. In this innocent not trying, non-doing... you can finally have communion with what is, with the rightness of who you are, with the fullness of Being and what you want to do now.

It's through letting now be enough you find Yourself; through innocent persistence you become Yourself. And what a mighty fine thing that is. The great Carl Jung sums it up nicely when he says, "The privilege of a lifetime is to become who you truly are".

One Last Thing

"Today is a good day to die."

— Lakota Sioux saying

This saying serves as a great reminder for me to make the most of my moments, to make the most of my day – it is a reminder not to compromise. It's so simple to take now for granted, isn't it? We think there'll always be more moments.

The greatest bringer of focus in life is death. The end really brings everything to a sharp point, doesn't it?

Memento Mori: this is a Latin phrase that means, "Remember that you will die". While we don't know how much time we might have, we certainly tend to waste time like we'll live forever.

If you knew how short life actually is, how would you live yours? No matter how uncertain or scared you might be, what would you start doing? What would you stop compromising on? What would you stop waiting for?

Realising that there is an unavoidable end puts the chase for more well in perspective doesn't it? And that's the whole point of this book: perspective. It's not about giving up more, but the ultimate celebration of the one moment you certainly have. This one.

We are truly blessed, but it is a choice to appreciate that or not. And so many of us do not.

Fulfilment is our choice. When you make the most of that choice, it truly means today becomes a great day to die. It becomes a day lived fully, completely, drinking it all in – and not just skimmed, fast-forwarded, ignored in a blaze of multi-tasking "efficiency", of trying to get there without any appreciation of where we are.

It's a reminder to not give my day to the urgent little tasks, but to soak in the truly important: that which nourishes my connection with Being and enables quality of doing. Now is not the time to indulge in petty complaints, to whine, to fritter on the irrelevant. So much life is lost to the un-important, the uncontrollable.

This is a beautiful world we live in, and this life is precious, it really is. Contentment really isn't complacency. It's the perfect invitation to enjoy more.

So – here's to the game of remembering to truly live. There's nothing to lose and yet everything to gain.

Go well.

"Be content with what you have;
rejoice in the way things are.

When you realise there is nothing lacking,
the whole world belongs to you."

— Lao Tzu

"One of the greatest appreciations I have for the Creator is the fact that there is always more coming to us, always, always more, it never ends being more."

— Maharishi Krishnananda Ishaya,
Teacher of the Bright Path Ishayas

QUOTE SOURCES

So much gratitude to the great teachers, authors and souls that have inspired me. I've quoted many, and want to acknowledge the source of their words.

Agassi, Andre, Open: An Autobiography, (HarperCollins, 2010).

Angelou, Maya, "People will forget...", source unknown, perhaps attributed.

Baldwin, James, Nobody Knows My Name: More Notes of a Native Son, (Penguin Modern Classics, 1991).

Buddha, "You only suffer...", source unknown, perhaps attributed.

Campbell, Joseph, A Joseph Campbell Companion: Reflections on the Art of Living, (HarperCollins, 1991).

Csikszentmihalyi, Mihaly, Flow: The Psychology of Happiness, (Rider, 2002).

Divine, Mark, "Josh Mantz: Trauma, the military and overcoming", Unbeatable Mind Podcast with Mark Divine, podcast #234, 28 November 2019, see: https://unbeatablemind.com/podcast/

Easwaran, Eknath, (Trans.), The Bhagavad Gita (Easwaran's Classics of Indian Spirituality), (Nilgiri Press, 2009).

Ferriss, Tim, "Brené Brown – Striving versus Self-Acceptance, Saving Marriages, and More", The Tim Ferriss Show, podcast #409, 6 February 2020, https://tim.blog/2020/02/06/brene-brown-striving-self-acceptance-saving-marriages/

Gandhi, "Be the change...", source unknown, perhaps attributed.

Heller, Joseph. Told by Bogle, John, in Enough, Georgetown University commencement, 18 May 2007, see: http://johncbogle.com/

wordpress/wp-content/uploads/2007/05/Georgetown_2007.pdf

Holiday, Ryan, "How Does It Feel To Get Everything You Ever Wanted?", Ryan Holiday – Meditations on Strategy and Life, 25 February 2020, see: https://ryanholiday.net/how-does-it-feel-to-get-everything-you-ever-wanted/

Ishaya, Maharishi Krishnananda, The Bright Path Ishayas live online session, 18 October 2020.

Ishaya, Maharishi Krishnananda, The Bright Path Ishayas live online session, 21 February 2021.

Jung, Carl, Modern Man in Search of a Soul, (Routledge, 2001).

Jung, Carl, "The privilege of...", source unknown, perhaps attributed.

Katie, Byron and Mitchell, Stephen, A Thousand Names For Joy: How To Live In Harmony With The Way Things Are, (Rider, 2007).

Kornfield, Jack, "Jack Kornfield – How to Find Peace Amidst COVID-19, How to Cultivate Calm in Chaos", The Tim Ferriss Show, podcast #414, 9 May 2020, see: https://tim.blog/2020/05/09/jack-kornfield-covid19-transcript/

Kotler, Steven. "Steven Kotler – Achieving Flow State and The Science Behind It", The Natural State with Dr. Anthony Gustin, podcast #129, 1 February 2021, see: https://dranthonygustin.libsyn.com/129-steven-kotler-achieving-flow-state-and-the-science-behind-it

Lakota Sioux, "Today is a...", source unknown, perhaps attributed.

Luther King, Jr., Martin, The Drum Major Instinct, Sermon Delivered at Ebenezer Baptist Church, Atlanta US, 4 February 1968, see: https://kinginstitute.stanford.edu/king-papers/documents/drum-major-instinct-sermon-delivered-ebenezer-baptist-church

Marcus, Aubrey, "After A Week In Darkness & Silence", Aubrey Marcus Podcast, podcast #243, 5 February 2020, see: https://www.

aubreymarcus.com/blogs/aubrey-marcus-podcast/sss

McGraw, Phil, Self Matters: Creating Your Life from the Inside Out, (Free Press, 2001).

Medaris Miller, Anna, "Olympic athletes say they face 'an epidemic' of suicide and depression in Michael Phelps' HBO documentary", Insider, 30 July 2020, see: https://www.insider.com/michael-phelps-weight-of-gold-olympians-suicide-depression-epidemic-2020-7

Nietzsche, Friedrich, "Joy is the...", source unknown, perhaps attributed.

Nietzsche, Friedrich & Hollingdale, R. J. (Trans.), Thus Spoke Zarathustra, (Penguin Classics, 1974).

Nietzsche, Friedrich & Kaufman, W. (Trans.), Basic Writings of Nietzsche, (Random House, 2001).

NIV Holy Bible (New International Version), Luke 9:25, (Hodder & Stoughton, 2015).

Osho, The Book of Understanding: Creating Your Own Path to Freedom, (Harmony, 2006).

Pascal, Blaise, Levi, A. (Ed.) & Levi, H. (Trans.), Pens'ees and Other Writings, (OUP Oxford, 2008).

Peterson, Jordan, 12 Rules for Life: An Antidote to Chaos, (Penguin, 2019).

Pressfield, Steven, Turning Pro: Tap Your Inner Power and Create Your Life's Work, (Black Irish Entertainment, 2012).

Quindlen, Anna, Anna Quindlen's Commencement Address at Villanova, Villanova University commencement, 23 June 2000, see: http://www.cs.oswego.edu/~wender/quindlen.html

Rumi & Barks, C. (Trans.), The Essential Rumi, (HarperCollins,

1995).

Seale, Ervin, Take Off from Within, (Devorss & Co., 1993).

Seneca & Romm, James S. (Trans.), How to Keep Your Cool: An Ancient Guide to Anger Management (Ancient Wisdom for Modern Readers), (Princeton University Press, 2019).

Serenity Prayer of the Alcoholics Anonymous, written by Reinhold Niebuhr, see: https://en.wikipedia.org/wiki/Serenity_Prayer

Stone, Oliver, Wall Street, (American Entertainment Partners/ Amercent Films, 1987).

Tzu, Lao, Feng, G. & English, J. (Trans.), Tao Te Ching, (Penguin, 1974).

Wachowski, Lilly & Wachowski, Lana, The Matrix, (Warner Bros. Pictures, 1999).

Walker, Brian. (Trans.), Hua Hu Ching: The Unknown Teachings of Lao Tzu, (HarperCollins, 1995).

Watts, Alan, "A scholar tries...", source unknown, perhaps attributed.

Wheal, Jamie, "Fat Shaming Time", Flow Genome Project, 18 February 2021, see: https://www.flowgenomeproject.com/post/fat-shaming-time

Wooden, John, Wooden: A Lifetime of Observations and Reflections On and Off the Court, (McGraw-Hill Education, 1997).

ABOUT THE AUTHOR

Originally an outdoor instructor from New Zealand, Arjuna Ishaya has been a Bright Path Ishaya monk and teacher since 2003.

Arjuna's aim is to make spirituality accessible for real people – not only as a tool for inner freedom and enlightenment, but to make peace practical so people can get what they want from life while having the most fun possible.

He is the author of 200% – An Instruction Manual for Living Life Fully, and is currently working with the British military and Metropolitan Police bomb disposal squads.

Arjuna lives in Richmond, North Yorkshire, UK with his wife and two children. He still gets out kayaking as much as he can.

www.arjunaishaya.com

www.thebrightpath.com

WOULD YOU…

If you enjoyed this book, would you take the time to positively review it?

Your review really makes a difference – it helps other people find good books. It's always been via the recommendation of others that I've picked up some life changing reading. So – much gratitude to you, in advance!

WANT MORE?

If you want more, I have an email list that I write to weekly. My goal is to encourage and support you on an inner journey, one that enhances every aspect of your outer life.

If that's of interest, and to stay in informed about the latest podcasts, books, courses and events, sign up here:

www.arjunaishaya.com/108ways-to-more

Talk more soon.

Lightning Source UK Ltd.
Milton Keynes UK
UKHW021003270921
391255UK00005B/247

9 781913 170981